BLACKSTONE'S

CIVIL
PRACTICE

BLACKSTONE'S

CIVIL PRACTICE

2008

UPDATING SUPPLEMENT

EDITOR-IN-CHIEF

HIS HONOUR JUDGE WILLIAM ROSE

EDITORS

STUART SIME
DEREK FRENCH

CONTRIBUTORS

EVAN ASHFIELD, JULIE BRANNAN
STUART BRIDGE, IAIN COLVILLE, ADRIAN KEANE
ANDREW LIDBETTER, ALAN OWENS
CHARLES PLANT, MICHAEL WALKER
MATTHEW WEINIGER, IVOR WEINTROUB
ANGELA WRIGHT

OXFORD
UNIVERSITY PRESS

OXFORD
UNIVERSITY PRESS

Great Clarendon Street, Oxford OX2 6DP

Oxford University Press is a department of the University of Oxford.
It furthers the University's objective of excellence in research, scholarship,
and education by publishing worldwide in

Oxford   New York

Auckland   Cape Town   Dar es Salaam   Hong Kong   Karachi
Kuala Lumpur   Madrid   Melbourne   Mexico City   Nairobi
New Delhi   Shanghai   Taipei   Toronto

With offices in

Argentina   Austria   Brazil   Chile   Czech Republic   France   Greece
Guatemala   Hungary   Italy   Japan   Poland   Portugal   Singapore
South Korea   Switzerland   Thailand   Turkey   Ukraine   Vietnam

Oxford is a registered trade mark of Oxford University Press
in the UK and in certain other countries

Published in the United States
by Oxford University Press Inc., New York

© Oxford University Press 2007

British Library Cataloguing in Publication Data

Data available

Library of Congress Cataloging in Publication Data

Data available

Typeset by RefineCatch Limited, Bungay, Suffolk
Printed in Great Britain
on acid-free paper by
Ashford Colour Press Ltd., Gosport, Hampshire

ISBN 978–0–19–923859–0

1 3 5 7 9 10 8 6 4 2

Introduction

This supplement updates *Blackstone's Civil Practice 2008* and follows the headings and the paragraph numbering used in that edition. This supplement was completed on 5 September 2007. Unless otherwise stated, all changes to legislation, rules, practice directions and court fees considered in this supplement came into force on 1 October 2007.

Please visit the *Blackstone's Civil Practice 2008* companion website at *www.oup.com/ blackstones/civil*, where this supplement is also available.

Contents

Table of Cases

Table of Primary Legislation

References are to Paragraph and Page Numbers

Table of Secondary Legislation

References are to Paragraph and Page Numbers

Supplement to Procedural Checklists

All changes to court fees came into force on 1 October 2007 (Civil Proceedings Fees (Amendment) (No. 2) Order 2007 (SI 2007/2176)).

Procedural checklist 5   Claim under standard Part 8 procedure

Fee	CPFO, fee 1.4, is now fee 1.5. The amount is unchanged.
Listing fee	CPFO, fee 2.2, is now £100 in both the county court and High Court.
Hearing fee	A multi-track hearing fee of £1,000 is payable with the listing fee (CPFO, fee 2.3).

Procedural checklist 6   Application for joinder

Fee	CPFO, fee 2.5, is now fee 2.6 and is £75 in both the county court and High Court. CPFO, fee 2.6, is now fee 2.7 and is £40 in both the county court and High Court.
After the hearing	CPFO, fee 1.5, is now fee 1.6 and is £40 in both the county court and High Court.

Procedural checklist 7   Interpleader proceedings: High Court

Fee	CPFO, fee 2.5, is now fee 2.6 and is £75. CPFO, fee 1.4, is now fee 1.5, but the amount is unchanged.

Procedural checklist 9   Approval of settlement or compromise to which a child or patient is party, where sole purpose of claim is to obtain court approval

Fee	For 'patient' read 'protected person'. PD 21, paras 6.1 and 6.2, are now PD 21, para. 5.1. PD 21, para. 6.3, is now PD 21, para. 5.2. PD 21, para. 6.5, is now PD 21, para. 5.6.
Hearing	In proceedings involving a child, the application will normally be heard by a master or district judge (PD 21, para. 5.6(1)). In proceedings involving a protected person, the proceedings will normally be heard by a master, designated civil judge or his nominee (PD 21, para. 5.6(2)). In the Chancery Division, the application will be heard by a judge if the amount exceeds £100,000 (PD 2B, para. 5.1(a)).

Procedural checklist 10   Application to extend time for service of claim form

Fee	CPFO, fee 2.6, is now fee 2.7 and is £40 in both the county court and High Court.

Procedural checklist 11   Application for permission to serve claim form out of jurisdiction

Application	Fee 1.7 is now fee 1.8. Fee 2.6 is now fee 2.7.
Fees	The fee is now £40 in both the county court and High Court (CPFO, fees 1.8(a) and 2.7).

Procedural checklist 12   Admitting a claim and requesting time to pay

	CPFO, notes to fee 2.6, now CPFO, notes to fee 2.7.

Procedural checklist 14 Procedure for disputing the court's jurisdiction

Fee   CPFO, fee 2.5, is now fee 2.6 and is £75 in both the county court and High Court.

Procedural checklist 15 Request for entry of judgment in default

CPFO, notes to fee 2.6, now CPFO, notes to fee 2.7.

Procedural checklist 16 Application for entry of judgment in default

Fee   CPFO, fee 2.5, is now fee 2.6 and is £75 in both the county court and High Court.

CPFO, fee 2.6, is now fee 2.7 and is £40 in both the county court and High Court.

Procedural checklist 19 Interim application without notice

Fee   CPFO, fee 2.6, is now fee 2.7 and is £40 in both the county court and High Court.

Procedural checklist 20 Interim application with notice

Fee   CPFO, fee 2.5, is now fee 2.6 and is £75 in both the county court and High Court.

Procedural checklist 22 Application by party for summary judgment

Fee   CPFO, fee 2.5, is now fee 2.6 and is £75 in both the county court and High Court.

Procedural checklist 24 Application for an order for interim payment

Fee   CPFO, fee 2.5, is now fee 2.6 and is £75 in both the county court and High Court.

Procedural checklist 26 Specific disclosure

Issue application   CPFO, fee 2.5, is now fee 2.6 and is £75 in both the county court and High Court.

Procedural checklist 27 Non-party disclosure

Issue application   CPFO, fee 2.5, is now fee 2.6 and is £75 in both the county court and High Court.

Procedural checklist 28 Trial preparation

Witness summonses   CPFO, fee 2.7, is now fee 2.8 and is £35 in both the county court and High Court.

Procedural checklist 33 Appeals within the county courts and High Court

Fee   CPFO, fees 2.3 and 2.4, are now fees 2.4 and 2.5, respectively, but the amounts are unchanged.

Respondent's notice CPFO, fees 2.3 and 2.4, are now fees 2.4 and 2.5, respectively, but the amounts are unchanged.

Supplement to Chapters 1–98

Chapter 1   The Overriding Objective and Sources of Procedural Law

THE CIVIL PROCEDURE RULES 1998

A new procedural code

Scope of the CPR: CPR, r. 2.1(2), is amended with effect from 1 October 2007 to change **1.10** the authority for the exclusion of Court of Protection proceedings (which remain excluded) from the Mental Health Act 1983, s. 106, to the Mental Capacity Act 2005, s. 51.

Old cases as a guide to principle

Nomura International plc v Granada Group Ltd [2007] EWHC 642 (Comm), [2007] 1 CLC 479. The **1.22** claim form had been issued at a time when the claimant had not decided to pursue a claim against the defendant, and had issued the claim form merely to protect its position. Cooke J made the point that pre-CPR authorities are not generally of relevance under the CPR. It is different where a CPR provision (here it was r. 16.2(1)) follows the same form and has the same intention as a provision in the RSC (in this case ord. 6, r. 2). In these situations the court should have regard to the principles that had informed the pre-CPR case law.

The same approach was taken in *Adelson v Associated Newspapers Ltd* [2007] EWCA Civ 701, *The Times*, 18 July 2007, in the context of an application to substitute a party after the expiry of limitation under CPR, r. 19.5(3)(a). This gives effect to the Limitation Act 1980, s. 35, with the same intention as the old provision in RSC, ord. 20, r. 5. Post-CPR cases (*Morgan Est (Scotland) Ltd v Hanson Concrete Products Ltd* [2005] EWCA Civ 134, [2005] 1 WLR 2557, and *Weston v Gribben* [2006] EWCA Civ 1425, [2007] CP Rep 10), which sought to lay down principles free of the pre-CPR case law, were doubted, and the court followed the principles laid down by the pre-CPR authorities.

A similar approach was also taken in relation to the address for service of a defendant while temporarily out of the jurisdiction in *City and Country Properties Ltd v Kamali* [2006] EWCA Civ 1879, [2007] 1 WLR 1219. The Court of Appeal overruled *Chellaram v Chellaram (No. 2)* [2002] EWHC 632 (Ch), [2002] 3 All ER 17, para [47], as inconsistent with *Rolph v Zolan* [1993] 1 WLR 1305.

Chapter 6   Conditional Fee Agreements

ENTERING INTO A CFA

Failure to comply with the Regulations

Disclosure of the CFA   *Brunton v Travel West Midlands Ltd* (Birmingham County Court 2007) **6.9** LTL 15/6/2007). Held it was legitimate and consistent with the overriding objective for a paying party to make a Part 18 request for further information as to the existence of legal expenses insurance. This went to the issues of whether ATE insurance was properly incurred, and whether there had been compliance with the Conditional Fee Agreements Regulations 2000 (SI 2000/692), reg. 4(2)(c).

London and Cambridge Properties Ltd v Bradbury (Kingston-upon-Hull County Court 2007) LTL 29/5/ 2007. There is no automatic right to disclosure of documents relating to possible compliance or otherwise with the CFA Regulations. In this case there was nothing available to doubt the integrity of the signature of the receiving party's solicitors, as officers of the court, indicating that the bill was accurate and complete, so disclosure was refused.

COLLECTIVE CONDITIONAL FEE AGREEMENTS

6.26 *Various Claimants v Gower Chemicals Ltd* (Cardiff County Court 2007) LTL 8/3/2007. A clause in a collective CFA requiring the claimants' solicitors to prepare and retain written risk assessments was held to be an innominate term. The Collective Conditional Fee Agreements Regulations 2000 (SI 2000/2988), reg. 5(1), required compliance with the specified particulars in the form of the agreement, but did not require performance of those specifications.

Chapter 7 Community Legal Service

WITHDRAWAL OF FUNDING

7.27 In the LSC, the title 'regional director' has been changed to 'director'.

Chapter 9 Notices before Action

ROAD TRAFFIC CASES

Untraced drivers

9.5 *Byrne v Motor Insurers Bureau* [2007] EWHC 1268 (QB), [2007] 3 All ER 499. In order to comply with Directive 84/5/EEC, the untraced drivers' agreement has to be taken as subject to a similar extension to the time limit for bringing a claim as that contained in the Limitation Act 1980, s. 28. The result is that time does not run against a child until he reaches the age of 18.

Chapter 10 Limitation

LIMITATION PERIODS

Breach of trust

10.4 *Halton International Inc (Holdings) Sàrl v Guernroy Ltd* [2005] EWHC 1968 (Ch), [2006] 1 BCLC 78. A voting agreement between shareholders under which a director was given power of attorney to act, in its absolute discretion, as the agent of and to vote the shares of the other shareholders, gave rise to a bare promise, not a trust. A claim based on allegations of a failure to exercise those powers in good faith and not to make secret profits was therefore governed by the usual six-year limitation period, and was not governed by the Limitation Act 1980, s. 21(1)(b).

Mortgages and deeds

Gotham v Doodes [2006] EWCA Civ 1080, [2007] 1 WLR 86. A charge on a bankrupt's dwelling **10.10** house in favour of the trustee in bankruptcy created by an order under the Insolvency Act 1986, s. 313, secures a future obligation, with no immediate right to receive any principal sum. Accordingly, time cannot run under the Limitation Act 1980, s. 20(1), until an order has been made for the sale of the property.

ACCRUAL OF CAUSE OF ACTION

Date of knowledge: significant injury

Young v South Tyneside Metropolitan Borough Council [2006] EWCA Civ 1534, [2007] 2 WLR 1192. **10.25** This was a negligence claim alleging psychiatric injury as a result of abuse by the defendant's employees. In deciding the date when the claimant knew he had suffered a significant injury, a substantially objective approach is required. This is answered applying the standard of the reasonable behaviour of a person who has suffered the degree of injury suffered by the claimant and which the claimant knew he had suffered. Subjective matters such as the claimant's intelligence, personal history and other personal characteristics are disregarded. Exceptionally, the court can take into account as a factor that a person who has suffered a particular type of injury may be reasonably inhibited from starting a claim. On the facts, the abuse was suffered in the 1970s, its nature did inhibit starting a claim, but the repression of the claimant's knowledge that he had suffered a significant injury ended after a chance meeting in 1996 with one of those alleged to be responsible.

McCoubrey v Ministry of Defence [2007] EWCA Civ 17, [2007] 1 WLR 1544. The key question is whether the claimant knew he had suffered a significant injury. Its effect on his career or private life is irrelevant under s. 14.

Date of knowledge: attributable to defendant's conduct

Secretary of State for Trade and Industry v Mackie [2007] EWCA Civ 642, LTL 28/6/2007. In 1992 the **10.26** claimant, a miner, took a hearing test and was informed he had suffered a 9.98 dB hearing loss. He was aware that other miners were making noise exposure claims against their employer on the basis of hearing losses of 10 dB. He was informed by a union official that he did not have a claim. He did not bring proceedings until after consulting solicitors in 2003. It was held that time ran from 1992, as the original hearing test was plainly arranged with a view to bringing a claim for damages, and showed an injury which was attributable to his working conditions. Even if the misinformation provided by the union official had displaced that knowledge, it was unreasonable for the claimant to do nothing for the next 10 years for the purposes of the Limitation Act 1980, s. 14(3).

CALCULATING THE LIMITATION PERIOD

Limitation and the date of issue

Barnes v St Helens Metropolitan Borough Council [2006] EWCA Civ 1372, [2007] 1 WLR 879. The **10.32** Court of Appeal drew a distinction between the date a claim is 'brought' (the word used in the Limitation Act 1980) and the date it is issued (the word used in the CPR). The result is that time stops running for limitation when the claim form and issue fee are delivered to the court (this is the date the claim is 'brought'), which is in the claimant's control, rather than the date of issue, over which the claimant does not have control.

Fraud

10.34 *Barnstaple Boat Co. Ltd v Jones* [2007] EWCA Civ 727, LTL 17/7/2007. While the claimant may have suspected the defendant's dishonesty at an earlier stage, the Limitation Act 1980, s. 32, requires knowledge of the fraud, not mere suspicion. As a result the claim, which was based on fraudulent misrepresentation, was not time-barred.

Concealment

10.35 *J. D. Wetherspoon plc v Van de Berg and Co. Ltd* [2007] EWHC 1044 (Ch), [2007] PNLR 28. Time did not run until the defendant's concealment could with reasonable diligence have been discovered.

Defamation: discretionary extension

10.44 *Edwards v Golding* [2007] EWCA Civ 416, *The Times*, 22 May 2007. Defamation claims accrue on publication, and knowledge of the identity of the publisher is not an essential element of the cause of action. Personal injuries claims are a special case (see Limitation Act 1980, ss. 11 and 14).

Chapter 11   Where to Start Proceedings

SPECIALIST CLAIMS

11.7 For Companies Act applications, old PD 49B has been replaced by PD 49 and new PD 49B. PD 49 deals with applications under the Companies Act 2006 as well as the Companies Act 1985 and related legislation.

Chapter 12   Issuing Proceedings

ISSUING A CLAIM FORM

12.3 *Barnes v St Helens Metropolitan Borough Council* [2006] EWCA Civ 1372, [2007] 1 WLR 879. The court staff who receive a claim form, fee etc. for the purpose of issue are not performing any judicial function, and have no power to reject the documents (at [19]). If the claim form is very defective, such as through not naming any parties, or not including any details of the claim, it may be rejected on the basis that it is not a claim form at all (per Tuckey LJ).

Chapter 14   Joinder and Parties

ADDITION AND SUBSTITUTION OF PARTIES

Principles

14.3 *Prescott v Dunwoody Sports Marketing* [2007] EWCA Civ 461, *The Times*, 25 May 2007. A court may substitute a new party for an existing one under CPR, r. 19.2(4), if the existing party's interest or liability has passed to the new party, provided it is desirable to make the order '... so that the court can resolve the matters in dispute in the proceedings' (r. 19.2(4))(b)). There was some dispute on the authorities as to whether this power remained open after judgment (*Kooltrade Ltd v XTS Ltd* [2002] FSR 49 suggested there was no such power, and *C Inc. plc v L* [2001] 2 Lloyd's Rep 459 and *The Selby Paradigm* [2004] EWHC 1804 (Admlty), [2004] 2 Lloyd's Rep 714, which suggested there was such a power, at least if there remained an issue between the parties). The dispute was resolved in favour of allowing such substitutions, with the transferee of the claimant's business being substituted after a final injunction was granted.

Addition or substitution of a party after the expiry of the limitation period

Correcting a mistake   *Adelson v Associated Newspapers Ltd* [2007] EWCA Civ 701, *The Times*, 18 **14.9** July 2007. This was an application to substitute a party after the expiry of limitation under CPR, r. 19.5(3)(a), which gives effect to the Limitation Act 1980, s. 35, with the same intention as the old provision in RSC, ord. 20, r. 5. It was therefore necessary to have regard to the pre-CPR principles in applying CPR, r. 19.5(3)(a). Post-CPR cases (*Morgan Est (Scotland) Ltd v Hanson Concrete Products Ltd* [2005] EWCA Civ 134, [2005] 1 WLR 2557, and *Weston v Gribben* [2006] EWCA Civ 1425, [2007] CP Rep 10), which sought to lay down principles free of the pre-CPR caselaw, were doubted. Accordingly, in these applications:

(a) The court must be satisfied that the person who makes the mistake, directly or through an agent, was the person responsible for issuing the claim form (r. 19.5(3)(a)).

(b) The applicant has to show that, had the mistake not been made, the new party would have been named in the claim form.

(c) The mistake has to be as to the name of the party rather than as to the identity of the party (*The Sardinia Sulcis* [1991] 1 Lloyd's Rep 201). This may be demonstrated if there was a mistake made about the group structure or the roles played by members of the group of companies in which the defendant and the new party operate; and no injustice should be caused if the application is granted. Often there will be a connection between the party named in the claim form and the party to be substituted (although this is not a requirement), and often the party intended to be substituted will have been aware of the proceedings (again this is not a formal requirement). If the party to be substituted was unaware of the claim, the court is likely to exercise its discretion against granting the application (*Horne-Roberts v SmithKline Beecham plc* [2001] EWCA Civ 2006, [2002] 1 WLR 1662).

Broadhurst v Broadhurst [2007] EWHC 1828 (Ch), LTL 10/4/2007. This first-instance case pre-dated *Adelson v Associated Newspapers Ltd* [2007] EWCA Civ 701, *The Times*, 18 July 2007. It makes the point (which must be right, and contradicts *Morgan Est (Scotland) Ltd v Hanson Concrete Products Ltd* [2005] EWCA Civ 134, [2005] 1 WLR 2557) that the use of 'substituted' in r. 19.5(3)(a) as opposed to 'added or substituted' in r. 19.5(3)(b) is significant. It means that a pure addition of a party is not permitted under r. 19.5(3)(a).

ABB Asea Brown Boveri Ltd v Hiscox Dedicated Corporate Member Ltd [2007] EWHC 1150 (Comm), LTL 24/5/2007. Under CPR, r. 17.4(3), the court has power to permit an amendment after the expiry of limitation to correct a mistake as to the name of a party, but only where the mistake is genuine and not one which could cause reasonable doubt as to the identity of the party in question. Whether a mistake would cause reasonable doubt as to the identity of the party intending to sue has to be determined objectively having regard to what is said in the claim form in the light of what was known by the defendant and the context in which the claim was made. A description of the role played by the claimant in the particulars of claim attached to the claim form may be sufficiently clear to avoid such doubt (*International Bulk Shipping and Services Ltd v Minerals and Metals Trading Corporation of India* [1996] 1 All ER 1017).

CHILDREN AND PATIENTS

Introduction

14.32 **Patients replaced by 'protected parties'** As from 1 October 2007 a patient is to be referred to as a 'protected party', in accordance with the Mental Capacity Act 2005. Changes are made to CPR, Part 21 (which is reissued, and renamed as 'Children and Protected Parties'). A protected party is a party, or intended party, who lacks capacity within the meaning of the Mental Capacity Act 2005 to conduct proceedings (r. 21.1(2)(c) and (d)). Like patients before them, protected parties must act through litigation friends (r. 21.2(1)). A deputy appointed by the Court of Protection under the Mental Capacity Act 2005 with power to conduct proceedings on the protected party's behalf is entitled to be the party's litigation friend in the relevant proceedings (r. 21.4(2)). A deputy intending to act as a litigation friend must file an official copy of the order of the Court of Protection when the claim form is issued or (if acting for a defendant) on first taking a step in the proceedings (r. 21.5(2)). In the absence of such a deputy, r. 21.4(3) continues to permit a person who can fairly and competently conduct proceedings on the protected party's behalf, who has no adverse interest, and who (if acting for a claimant) undertakes to pay any costs the protected party may be ordered to pay, to act as the protected party's litigation friend. Such a person needs to file and serve a certificate of suitability (r. 21.5(3) and (4)).

Where money is recovered by or on behalf of a protected party, before giving directions under r. 21.11(2) for the investment (or otherwise) of that money, the court must consider whether the protected party is a protected beneficiary (r. 21.11(3)). This is a protected party who lacks capacity to manage and control money he recovers in the proceedings (r. 21.1(2)(e)).

Amendments are made in terminology to CPR, Part 6, and in particular to the table in r. 6.6(1). This now says that the person who must be served with a claim form where the defendant is a protected party must be either:

(a) the attorney under a registered enduring power of attorney; or

(b) the donee of a lasting power of attorney; or

(c) the deputy appointed by the Court of Protection; or

(d) if there is no such person, an adult with whom the protected party resides or in whose care the protected party is.

Changes in terminology to substitute 'protected party' for 'patient' are made in rr. 6.6, 12.10(a)(i), 12.11(3), 14.1(4), 30.7, 32.13(3)(e), 36.9(2), 39.2(3)(d), 45.10(2)(c), 46.1(2)(c), 47.3(1)(c) and Part 48.

The former r. 21.11A on the expenses incurred by a litigation friend is renumbered as r. 21.12, and the former r. 21.12 on the appointment of a guardian of a child's estate becomes r. 21.13.

COMPANIES

14.41 *Fusion Interactive Communication Solutions Ltd v Venture Investment Placement Ltd (No. 2)* [2005] EWHC 736 (Ch), [2005] 2 BCLC 571. Authorisation of litigation by the directors may in practical terms be frustrated if the board is evenly split, in cases where the articles of association do not provide for a casting vote. However, the courts will not permit directors to take advantage of their positions so as to block litigation against other companies in which they may have interests, because such conduct would be a breach of duty by the directors.

14.42 *Foss v Harbottle* **and derivative claims** A derivative claim is defined in the Companies Act 2006, s. 260(1), as a proceeding by a member of a company:

(a) in respect of a cause of action vested in the company, and

(b) seeking relief on behalf of the company.

In this provision, 'member' includes a person to whom shares in the company have been transferred, or have been transmitted by operation of law (that is, to a personal representative of a deceased member or the trustee of a bankrupt member), but who is not a member of the company (because of not being registered as the holder of the shares) (s. 260(5)(c)).

As from 1 October 2007, a derivative claim may be brought only under the Companies Act 2006, part 11, chapter 1 (ss. 260 to 264), or in pursuance of a court order under s. 996(2)(c) (protection of members against unfair prejudice) (s. 260(2)). The procedure on a derivative claim is governed by CPR, rr. 19.9 to 19.9F, but those rules do not apply to a claim authorised by the court under s. 996(2)(c) (CPR, r. 19.9(1)(b)). A derivative claim must be commenced by claim form (r. 19.9(2)), which must be headed 'Derivative claim' (PD 19C, para. 2(1)). The company must be joined as a co-defendant so that if its rights are vindicated it will be able to enforce the judgment (CPR, r. 19.9(3)).

A statutory derivative claim under the Companies Act 2006, ss. 260 to 264, may be brought only in respect of a cause of action specified in s. 260. The cause of action must be vested in the company (s. 260(1)). It must arise from an actual or proposed act or omission which involves negligence, default, breach of duty or breach of trust by a director, former director or shadow director of the company (s. 260(3) and (5)(a) and (b)). The cause of action may be against the director, or another person or both (s. 260(3)). It may have arisen before the claimant became a member of the company (s. 260(4)).

A member of a company who brings a statutory derivative claim under ss. 260 to 264 must apply to the court for permission to continue it (s. 261(1)). For the first time, s. 263 gives guidance on how the court should approach deciding whether to give permission. The principal matters to be taken into account are:

(a) whether the company has decided not to pursue the claim (s. 263(3)(e));

(b) the views of disinterested members (s. 263(4));

(c) whether the claim would promote the company's success (s. 263(2)(a) and (3)(b));

(d) whether there has been, or could be, authorisation or ratification of the act or omission giving rise to the claim (s. 263(2)(b) and (c) and (3)(c) and (d));

(e) the good faith of the derivative claimant (s. 263(3)(a)).

In response to fears that putting derivative claims on a statutory basis would lead to a flood of litigation, especially in respect of directors' negligence (for which derivative claims were not previously allowed unless the director had benefited personally from the wrongdoing), s. 261 requires the court to consider an application for permission to continue a derivative claim in two stages. At the first stage it considers only the evidence presented by the claimant and must dismiss the application if this evidence does not disclose a prima facie case for giving permission (s. 261(2)). If the court decides that there is a prima facie case, it will give directions for a contested hearing of the application (s. 261(3)).

When the claim form for a derivative claim is issued, the claimant must file an application notice under CPR, Part 23, for permission to continue the claim, together with written evidence in support (Companies Act 2006, s. 261(1); CPR, r. 19.9A(2)). The claimant must not take any further step in the proceedings (other than pursuing the permission application) without the court's permission, except for an urgent application for interim relief (r. 19.9(4)).

At the first stage the company must not be made a respondent to the permission application (r. 19.9A(3)) but must be given notice of it in accordance with r. 19.9A(4), (5) and (6), and PD 19C, para. 4. The court may, on a without-notice application by the claimant, order that the company need not be notified of the permission application, if notification would be likely to frustrate some part of the remedy sought (CPR, r. 19.9A(7) and (8)). An application for an order under r. 19.9A(7) must state the reasons for the application and any written evidence in support must be filed with it (PD 19C, para. 3).

A permission application in the High Court is assigned to the Chancery Division and will be decided by a judge. In a county court it will be decided by a circuit judge (PD 19C, para. 6).

At the first stage, the court must dismiss the permission application if it appears that the application and the supporting evidence do not disclose a prima facie case for giving permission (Companies Act 2006, s. 261(2)). A permission application may be dismissed on this basis without a hearing (CPR, r. 19.9A(9)). If so, the claimant may, within seven days of being notified of the decision, request an oral hearing to reconsider it (r. 19.9A(10)). Such a request must be in writing and must be notified to the company in writing, unless the court orders otherwise (r. 19.9A(10)). A decision at the first stage will normally be made without submissions from the company. If, without invitation by the court, the company volunteers a submission, or appears at an oral hearing, it will not normally be allowed its costs (PD 19C, para. 5).

If the court does not dismiss for failure to disclose a prima facie case, it will order that the company, and any other appropriate party, must be made respondents to the application, and give directions for service (CPR, r. 19.9A(12)) so that there can be a full hearing.

On a full hearing, the court may give permission to continue the derivative claim on such terms as it thinks fit, or refuse permission and dismiss the claim, or adjourn the proceedings and give such directions as it thinks fit (Companies Act 2006, s. 261(4)).

A person making a derivative claim on behalf of a company may seek indemnification by the company for the costs of the claim—see 66.51.

Continuation of a company's claim as a derivative claim or of a derivative claim with a different claimant

14.42A If those with authority to conduct a company's litigation fear a derivative claim, they may try to block it by causing the company to bring a claim but with no intention of genuinely pursuing it. The Companies Act 2006, s. 262, therefore permits a member of a company to apply to the court for permission to take over a claim brought by the company and continue it as a derivative claim on the grounds that:

(a) the manner in which the company commenced or continued the claim amounts to an abuse of the process of the court;

(b) the company has failed to prosecute the claim diligently; and

(c) it is appropriate for the member to continue the claim as a derivative claim.

There is a similar provision in s. 264, for an existing derivative claim to be taken over by a new claimant on the same grounds. An application for permission under s. 262 or s. 264 follows the same two-stage process as an application under s. 261. CPR, r. 19.9B, applies r. 19.9A with necessary modifications.

Permission to continue a derivative claim may be given on condition that the claim is not to be discontinued, settled or compromised without the court's permission (r. 19.9F). This will be appropriate to ensure that other members of the company are given an opportunity to continue the derivative claim themselves (PD 19C, para. 7).

CONSOLIDATION

14.58 *IXIS Corporate and Investment Bank v WestLB AG* [2007] EWHC 1748 (Comm), LTL 30/7/2007. This was an application to consolidate a claim in which the applicant was the claimant with another claim in which it was the defendant. The other parties in the two claims were different. Although there was a degree of overlap between the two cases, a trial date had been fixed in one case whereas the other had not reached the defence stage. It was therefore neither fair nor just to order consolidation.

VEXATIOUS LITIGANTS

Civil restraint orders

R (Kumar) v Secretary of State for Constitutional Affairs [2006] EWCA Civ 990, [2007] 1 WLR 536. In   **14.70** considering whether to make a civil restraint order the court is entitled to take into account any proceedings and applications made by the respondent which the court considers to be totally without merit. It is not restricted to proceedings and applications where there was at the time an express finding of a total lack of merit.

Chapter 15   Filing and Service

EXTENDING TIME FOR SERVING A CLAIM FORM

Applications made after the usual period of service has expired

Carnegie v Drury [2007] EWCA Civ 497, *The Times*, 11 June 2007. On the last day for service, the   **15.10** claimant asked the second defendant's last employer (the first defendant) if it had instructions to accept service on behalf of the second defendant, and if not, for his address. Ten minutes before it expired, the claim form was faxed to the first defendant (which was effective service on the first defendant). After expiry, an extension was granted under CPR, r. 7.6(3). It was held that the extension should not have been granted, and that the judge made two substantial mistakes:

(a) in misunderstanding the facts, in thinking that the claimant had sent documents addressed to the second defendant at the first defendant's address, whereas no documents were enclosed; and

(b) in giving weight to efforts made by the claimant to effect service on the second defendant after the claim form had expired. It is only efforts made before expiry which are relevant under r. 7.6(3).

Further, exceptional circumstances, with a full explanation of what had been done, were required before the court could find that the claimant had acted promptly and in explaining delay when an application for an extension to a claim form was made after it had expired.

FILING DOCUMENTS

Inspecting the court file

Public right of access to court register and to court documents   *Sayers v SmithKline Beecham*   **15.16** *plc* [2007] EWHC 1346 (QB), LTL 31/7/2007. Various documents filed in the UK MMR/MR vaccine litigation were permitted to be released for use in litigation in the USA. The American courts could be trusted to impose suitable conditions on the use of the documents, and that anonymisation of confidential information in the released documents would be preserved.

WHO MAY SERVE DOCUMENTS?

15.19   Old PD 49B, para. 11, has been replaced by PD 49, para. 20. Neither the High Court nor a county court will serve documents in companies matters.

METHODS OF SERVICE

Address for service

15.24   *City and Country Properties Ltd v Kamali* [2006] EWCA Civ 1879, [2007] 1 WLR 1219. A claim form served at the defendant's address for service within the jurisdiction at a time when the defendant is temporarily outside the jurisdiction is valid service. This applies to defendants abroad on holiday or business, and even (based on the facts of *Rolph v Zolan* [1993] 1 WLR 1305) to a defendant who has emigrated where the claim form is sent to the defendant's last known address within the jurisdiction.

Chapter 16   Service Outside the Jurisdiction

CASES OUTSIDE THE GENERAL RULES

Under the Jurisdiction and Judgments Regulation

16.11   **Companies and associations**   *Speed Investments Ltd v Formula One Holdings Ltd* [2004] EWCA Civ 1512, [2005] 1 BCLC 455. A dispute over the composition of the board of a company fell within art. 22 of the Jurisdiction and Judgments Regulation, so that proceedings had to be commenced where the company had its seat. This was so even though the dispute arose out of the interpretation of a shareholders' agreement, and even though there was no live issue of English company law in the case.

JURISDICTION UNDER THE JURISDICTION AND JUDGMENTS REGULATION

Contract

16.25   **Jurisdiction agreements**   *Mazur Media Ltd v Mazur Media GmbH* [2004] EWHC 1566 (Ch), [2005] 1 BCLC 305. In this case the English court was held to have exclusive jurisdiction over certain claims by reason of a jurisdiction clause, but not over claims in tort, because the harm was done in Germany.

ASSUMED JURISDICTION

Basic principles governing applications for permission

16.44   *Langlands v SG Hambros Trust Co. (Jersey) Ltd* [2007] EWHC 627 (Ch), LTL 8/5/2007. Permission to serve outside the jurisdiction was refused because the central event of the alleged breach took place outside the jurisdiction, and there was no arguable claim. It was said it would be different if the relevant information on whether the grounds in CPR, rr. 6.20 and 6.21, are made out is in the hands of the defendant, but unavailable to the claimant.

INJUNCTIONS TO RESTRAIN FOREIGN PROCEEDINGS

Samengo-Turner v J and H Marsh and McLennan (Services) Ltd [2007] EWCA Civ 723, LTL 12/07/2007. **16.71**
Employers commenced proceedings in New York against employees under bonus agreements, which should have been started in England under the Jurisdiction and Judgments Regulation, art. 18. The New York court, applying its rules, held it had exclusive jurisdiction. The English Court of Appeal granted an anti-suit injunction to restrain the New York proceedings as the only way to prevent the New York court from proceeding, because it would not recognise the effect of art. 18.

Chapter 21   Acting by a Solicitor

AUTHORITY OF SOLICITORS

Fusion Interactive Communication Solutions Ltd v Venture Investment Placement Ltd (No. 2) [2005] **21.12**
EWHC 736 (Ch), [2005] 2 BCLC 571. This case deals with the effect on a defendant where conflicting letters of claim are sent by different firms of solicitors instructed by the same company. On the facts, compliance with one letter of claim meant that there was no default in respect of the second (and wider) claim as set out in the other letter.

Chapter 23   Claim Form

CONTENTS OF A CLAIM FORM

Brief details of claim

Nomura International plc v Granada Group Ltd [2007] EWHC 642 (Comm), [2007] 1 CLC 479. The **23.4**
claim form had been issued at a time when the claimant had not decided to pursue a claim against the defendant, and had issued the claim form merely to protect its position. Cooke J said that CPR, r. 16.2(1), followed the same form and had the same intention as RSC, ord. 6, r. 2. Therefore, he had regard to the principles that had informed the pre-CPR cases of *Sterman v E. W. and W. J. Moore* [1970] 1 QB 596 and *Marshall v London Passenger Transport Board* [1936] 2 All ER 83. These decided that failing to include a concise statement on what is now the claim form could only be cured if the claimant had a known and genuine cause of action when the claim was issued. Gaining such knowledge by the time the application to strike out was heard was not enough, and the claim was struck out.

Chapter 24   Particulars of Claim

STRUCTURE OF PARTICULARS OF CLAIM

Conticorp SA v Central Bank of Ecuador [2007] UKPC 40, LTL 20/6/2007. The ultimate purpose of a **24.8**
party's pleadings is to inform the other party of the case against him. In this particular case

the issues were convoluted, but were not in doubt, partly because further and better particulars (equivalent to further information under CPR, Part 18) had been provided.

Sinclair Investment Holdings SA v Versailles Trade Finance Ltd [2005] EWCA Civ 722, [2006] 1 BCLC 60. This was a claim for breach of fiduciary duty based on an assumption of a duty of loyalty (as opposed to the more usual director and trustee situations) with an alternative claim in constructive trust. Although the assumption of loyalty was not expressly pleaded, it was held to be sufficiently pleaded by allegations that the defendant controlled the exercise, or was in the position to control the exercise, of powers over the claimant's money.

English, Welsh and Scottish Railway Ltd v Goodman (2007) LTL 21/8/2007. This was a claim against a former employee for breach of restrictive covenants. The particulars of claim was pleaded in a general and non-specific way. It was struck out as far too broad in its claims and allegations, unfocused and unparticularised.

Dunn v Glass Systems (UK) Ltd (2007) LTL 23/7/2007. Particulars of claim which was 221 pages long was struck out because it was excessively long, contained details which were irrelevant to the cause of action, contained a large number of terms that were incomprehensible, and also contained privileged material.

Chapter 28   Counterclaims

PROCEDURE

28.3   CPFO, fee 1.6, is now fee 1.7. CPFO, fee 1.5, is now fee 1.6 and is now £40 in both county court and High Court.

Chapter 30   Further Information

REQUEST FOR FURTHER INFORMATION

30.2   *Harcourt v Griffin* [2007] EWHC 1500 (QB), LTL 19/7/2007. The claimant had a claim likely to be worth over £8 million against an unincorporated association which did not have a great deal of assets. He made a request for further information to disclose the nature and extent of the insurance cover available to meet his claim, as it would be irrational to devote a great deal of legal expense to maximising damages if the resources available were limited. While the level of insurance cover was not strictly 'a matter in dispute' between the parties, CPR, Part 18, should be construed liberally to enable the parties to have the information they needed to deal efficiently and justly with the dispute. Disclosure was accordingly ordered.

OBJECTIONS TO RESPONDING

30.5   *English, Welsh and Scottish Railway Ltd v Goodman* (2007) LTL 21/8/2007. This was a claim against a former employee for breach of restrictive covenants. The particulars of claim was pleaded in a general and non-specific way. It was struck out partly because the claimant refused to answer a request for further information on the ground, regarded as inadequate in the circumstances, that the answers would be found in the exchanged witness statements.

Chapter 31   Amendments to Statements of Case

PRINCIPLES ON WHICH PERMISSION IS GRANTED

Amendments with no real prospect of success

Giles v Rhind [2007] EWHC 687 (Ch), LTL 5/4/2007. In proceedings to set aside a transaction under **31.6** the Insolvency Act 1986, s. 423, the claimant sought to amend the particulars of claim to change the alleged date of a deed which he said set out the proportions in which the parties held certain property. The defence had alleged that the deed as originally pleaded was a sham, or was in fact made six years later, and after the relevant dispute arose. It was held that while there were serious questions as to the reliability and credibility of the claimant's evidence, this was not a case where the amended case was incredible, so permission to amend was granted.

Findlay v Cantor Index Ltd [2007] EWHC 643 (QB), LTL 20/4/2007. An amendment will be refused where the amended case has no real prospect of success. CPR, Part 24, can properly be relied upon to establish this (*Flexitallic Group Inc. v T and N Ltd* (2001) LTL 9/1/2002). Amendments were refused in *TG Can Ltd v Crown Packaging UK plc* [2007] EWHC 1271 (QB), LTL 1/6/2007, where the claimant sought to add implied terms to the particulars of claim. The court held that there was no basis, such as to give business efficacy to the contract, for implying the proposed terms.

AMENDMENT OF CAUSES OF ACTION AFTER EXPIRY OF LIMITATION

Same or substantially the same facts

Del Grosso v Payne and Payne [2007] EWCA Civ 340, LTL 1/3/2007. The original claim against the **31.18** defendant solicitors was based on alleged negligence in failing to advise the client on the effect of a break clause in a lease. It was held that a wide-ranging amendment to the particulars of claim, alleging new beaches of duty, issues relating to the scope of the retainer, and the basis of the alleged financial losses, did not arise out of the same or substantially the same facts as the original claim.

Charles Church Developments Ltd v Stent Foundations Ltd [2006] EWHC 3158 (TCC), [2007] 1 WLR 1203. *Goode v Martin* [2001] EWCA Civ 1899, [2002] 1 WLR 1828, was applied to permit a claimant to adopt facts after the expiry of limitation which had been pleaded by one defendant by amending the particulars of claim against the other defendant.

Chapter 32   Applications and Interim Orders

PRE-ACTION INTERIM REMEDIES

Seal v Chief Constable of South Wales Police [2007] UKHL 31, [2007] 1 WLR 1910. Held that the **32.5** failure to obtain leave under the Mental Health Act 1983, s. 139(2), before commencing proceedings based on police action in removing him to a place of safety under s. 136 rendered the proceedings a nullity.

Re Taylor [2006] EWHC 3029 (Ch), [2007] Ch 150. Proceedings commenced against a bankrupt without the leave required by the Insolvency Act, s. 285(3), were a nullity, and could not be retrieved by granting retrospective leave. See update note to 81.33.

Chapter 33   Striking Out

NO REASONABLE GROUNDS FOR BRINGING OR DEFENDING THE CLAIM

33.7   *Sinclair Investment Holdings SA v Versailles Trade Finance Ltd* [2005] EWCA Civ 722, [2006] 1 BCLC 60. This was a claim for breach of fiduciary duty based on an assumption of a duty of loyalty (as opposed to the more usual director and trustee situations) with an alternative claim in constructive trust. It was held that the assumption of loyalty element was sufficiently pleaded by allegations that the defendant controlled the exercise, or was in the position to control the exercise, of powers over the claimant's money. The constructive trust claim was pleaded in novel circumstances, but there was no authority against liability being established on the pleaded facts (which included actual fraud), so this was allowed to proceed.

ABUSE OF PROCESS

General examples of abuse of process

33.13   *Nomura International plc v Granada Group Ltd* [2007] EWHC 642 (Comm), [2007] 1 CLC 479. The claim form had been issued at a time when the claimant had not decided to pursue a claim against the defendant, and had issued the claim form merely to protect its position. Cooke J made the point that pre-CPR authorities are not generally of relevance, but where, as here, a CPR provision (r. 16.2(1)) followed the same form and had the same intention of a provision in the RSC (here ord. 6, r. 2), the court should have regard to the principles that had informed the pre-CPR caselaw. The relevant cases here were *Sterman v E. W. and W. J. Moore* [1970] 1 QB 596 and *Marshall v London Passenger Transport Board* [1936] 2 All ER 83. These decided that failing to include a concise statement on what is now the claim form could only be cured if the claimant had a known and genuine cause of action when the claim was issued. Gaining such knowledge by the time the application to strike out was heard was not enough, and the claim was struck out.

Chapter 34   Summary judgment

ORDERS AVAILABLE

34.9   *Costain Ltd v Wilson* [2007] EWHC 713 (QB), LTL 12/4/2007. It was held there was no real prospect of success on D2's defence on a claim to recover sums obtained from the claimant on false invoices, where the proceeds had been divided equally between D1 and D2. The claimant was in the process of negotiating a settlement with D1. In order to avoid double recovery, while the claimant was strictly entitled to judgment in the full amount against D2, summary judgment was entered for half that amount in order to set a realistic unarguable recovery target.

P and O Nedlloyd BV v Arab Metals Co. [2006] EWCA Civ 1717, [2007] 2 All ER (Comm) 401. On an application by a claimant for summary judgment, the court cannot dismiss the claim under PD 24, para. 5, without the claimant being put on notice (usually through a cross-application) and being given an opportunity to address the court and place before it any relevant material (per Moore-Bick LJ at [67]).

TEST FOR ENTERING SUMMARY JUDGMENT

Points of law and construction

ICI Chemicals and Polymers Ltd v TTE Training Ltd [2007] EWCA Civ 725, LTL 13/6/2007. This was a **34.14** claim for repayment of money paid to a training services company. The defence was that the claimant, defendant and a new training provider had entered into a novation to the effect that the new training provider stood in place of the defendant. The defence turned on the construction of the novation agreement. It was held that where a short point of construction arises on a summary judgment application, the judge should decide the point, unless there is likely to be other evidence available at trial which will shed light on the point of construction. As the parties were ready to argue the point fully, the court determined the point, and found that the liability had been transferred to the new training provider.

BBC Worldwide Ltd v Bee Load Ltd [2007] EWHC 134 (Comm), LTL 16/2/2007. Held that the court has jurisdiction to grant summary judgment in respect of declarations where the issue raised is purely one of construction.

Disputes of fact

Costain Ltd v Wilson [2007] EWHC 713 (QB), LTL 12/4/2007. This was a claim to recover sums **34.15** obtained from the claimant on false invoices, where the proceeds had been divided equally between a subcontractor and the claimant's accountants. The subcontractor sought to avoid summary judgment by alleging that four of the claimant's employees, whom the subcontractor refused to name, had also benefited from the fraud, and were the alter ego of the claimant. The fact these allegedly corrupt employees were not named, the absence of evidence that they had gained from the fraud, and the fact that it was not a defence to the subcontractor's own wrongdoing, meant this was a hopeless argument.

Negligence claims and previous convictions

Bishara v Sheffield Teaching Hospitals NHS Trust [2007] EWCA Civ 353, LTL 26/3/2007. It was not **34.16** appropriate to grant summary judgment to a defendant on the basis there was no duty of care in a novel situation, where the question of whether a duty of care was owed had to be decided in the light of all the facts and evidence (*Caparo Industries plc v Dickman* [1990] 2 AC 605; *Capital and Counties plc v Hampshire County Council* [1997] QB 1004).

Housing Grants, Construction and Regeneration Act 1996 claims

Lead Technical Services Ltd v CMS Medical Ltd [2007] EWCA Civ 316, LTL 30/1/2007. Summary **34.18** judgment on an adjudicator's award should not have been granted, because there was a real prospect that the defendant could prove that the original agreement between the parties had been supplanted by a signed deed of appointment which had the effect of depriving the adjudicator of jurisdiction.

Aveat Heating Ltd v Jerram Falkus Construction Ltd [2007] EWHC 131 (TCC), LTL 16/2/2007. A clause in a construction contract that provided that the adjudicator's decision was valid even if issued out of time meant that the Housing Grants, Construction and Regeneration Act 1996, s. 108(2)(c) and (d), had not been complied with. This meant that the provisions in the Scheme for Construction Contracts applied to the dispute.

Evidence not yet investigated

34.19 *Microsoft Corporation v P4 Com Ltd* [2007] EWHC 746 (Ch), LTL 23/4/2007. This was a claim for trade mark and copyright infringement during a specific 14-month period. The defendant sought summary judgment, relying on documentary evidence supporting its allegation that it had been a dormant company during that period. Summary judgment was refused, because the evidence adduced was simply that chosen by the defendant. Disclosure and cross-examination could be revelatory and could completely change the picture, and there was evidence even at this stage that the defendant had operated a website which could have been used to generate business for the allegedly infringing activities.

Amendment

34.23 *P and O Nedlloyd BV v Arab Metals Co.* [2006] EWCA Civ 1717, [2007] 2 All ER (Comm) 401. A respondent to an application for summary judgment cannot be strictly confined to what appears from his existing statement of case (per Moore-Bick LJ at [62]). If he wishes to rely on matters going beyond a filed statement of case, the court will need to consider whether to allow an amendment.

ADMISSIONS

Permission to withdraw or amend admissions

34.28 A party seeking to withdraw admissions made in statements of case must apply for permission (under CPR, rr. 14.1(5) and 17.3). In deciding whether to give permission, the court is required by PD 14, para. 7.2, to have regard to all the circumstances of the case, including a list of factors, which are then set out.

White v Greensand Homes Ltd [2007] EWCA Civ 643, *The Times*, 19 July 2007. In its defence, the defendant company admitted an allegation that it had designed the foundations for a building, and defended the claim on other grounds. After reviewing the matter, the defendant company found that the design work had been done by another contractor (a company that was dissolved three years before the current application), and applied to amend by withdrawing the admission.

The admission in the defence repeated the same admission which had been made in earlier correspondence. The admission in the letter was before the expiry of limitation; the original defence was after the expiry of limitation. If there had been no letter, the amendment would simply have been allowed, as there would have been no claim lost because of the admission. With the letter, there was potential prejudice to the claimant. The amendment should only be allowed if the claimant could be left in no worse position than if the amended defence had been served at the time of the original defence, and in no better position than if the claimant had applied to strike it out under CPR, r. 3.4(2)(b). Taking into account the risk of finding liability on a false basis, the chances of the claimant bringing a claim against the other contractor relying on the latent damage provisions, and the risk the other contractor may have been unable to pay at all stages, the balance favoured granting permission to withdraw the admission.

CROSS-CLAIMS

Set-offs

34.34 *Benford Ltd v Lopecan SL* [2004] EWHC 1897 (Comm), [2004] 2 Lloyd's Rep 618. An equitable set-off arises where there is a close commercial relationship between the parties. What is required is an 'inseparable connection'. It is not necessary for the claim and cross-claim to arise out of the same transaction, provided the cross-claim flowed from the dealings and transactions which gave rise to the subject matter of the claim.

Chapter 36   Interim Payments

GROUNDS

Woodfine Leeds Smith v Russell [2007] EWHC 603 (QB), LTL 8/5/2007. The claimant was a member **36.7** of a directors' pension fund, and obtained a determination from the Pensions Ombudsman requiring the scheme trustee to take steps to ensure the claimant received the benefits properly payable under the scheme. The claimant subsequently sued the solicitors who were acting for him at the time for failing to seek an interim payment on account of those benefits. In the negligence claim it was held that the circumstances fell outside the grounds laid down in CPR, Part 25, and it was pointed out that there was no clear or well-established basis for making an application for an interim payment in such circumstances. It is probably the case that there is no such basis, other than asking for a voluntary interim payment, in circumstances outside Part 25.

AMOUNT TO BE ORDERED

Spillman v Bradford Riding Centre [2007] EWHC 89 (QB), LTL 13/2/2007. This was a case where the **36.15** claimant suffered serious personal injuries, and the defendant was concerned that ordering a substantial interim payment would result in the claimant spending the money on accommodation and care which would then be almost bound to be awarded at trial. Applying CPR, r. 25.7(4), the judge decided:

(a) The time already elapsed and the time yet to elapse before trial were significant factors.
(b) The purpose behind ordering a 'reasonable proportion' of the likely award is to minimise prejudice to the defendant arising from an overpayment. In the instant case the defendant had accepted 70 per cent liability, and the reasonable proportion was 75 per cent of the total which in this case had been proposed by the defendant, less earlier interim payments.
(c) The purpose for which the payment was to be put did not affect the outcome.

Chapter 37   Interim Injunctions

EXCEPTIONAL CASES

Right to freedom of expression

Boehringer Ingelheim Ltd v Vetplus Ltd [2007] EWCA Civ 583, [2007] FSR 29. Damage to reputation **37.35** is not in itself enough to displace the usual rule under the Human Rights Act 1998, s. 12(3), that the claimant must show a case which will probably succeed at trial before an interim injunction will be granted which may interfere with the freedom of expression (*Cream Holdings Ltd v Banerjee* [2004] UKHL 44, [2005] 1 AC 253). Otherwise, the exceptions would be so wide that s. 12(3) would be rendered virtually meaningless.

Defamation claims at common law

37.36 *Boehringer Ingelheim Ltd v Vetplus Ltd* [2007] EWCA Civ 583, [2007] FSR 29. The defamation rule in *Bonnard v Perryman* [1891] 2 Ch 269 does not apply to trade mark infringement cases, even where the trade mark is used in comparative advertising.

THE ORDER

Operative provisions

37.54 *Huntingdon Life Sciences Group plc v Stop Huntingdon Animal Cruelty* [2007] EWHC 522 (QB), LTL 19/4/2007. A final injunction was granted restraining animal rights protestors from harassing the claimant's employees by establishing exclusion zones which were to be binding on all protestors, not only those who were members of the defendant association. 'Protestor' was defined in the order to mean:

(a) the defendants, whether by themselves, their servants [employees] or agents; and

(b) any other person, whether by himself, his servants or agents, who was acting in concert with the defendant with a view to exposing, deterring, obstructing or preventing the conduct of experimentation on live animals by the claimant; but

(c) not to be enforceable against any individual without the express permission of the court.

In respect of the main site, there was provision for a maximum of 30 protestors, responsible dropping-off or picking-up at the protest site, an off-road parking place to be found in the vicinity of the protest site, megaphones to be permitted for a maximum of one hour at medium to low amplification for verbal sound, and a protest procession to be allowed every three months.

Similar cases are *RWE Npower plc v Carrol* [2007] EWHC 947 (QB), LTL 9/5/2007 (where there was an unincorporated protest group who had engaged 'professional protestors' to prevent the development of a new power station); and *SmithKline Beecham plc v Avery* [2007] EWHC 948 (QB), LTL 9/5/2007 (an animal rights protest case).

Chapter 38   Freezing Injunctions

CONDITIONS FOR GRANTING FREEZING INJUNCTIONS

Good arguable case

38.7 *Fiona Trust Holding Corporation v Privalov* [2007] EWHC 1217 (Comm), LTL 30/5/2007. David Steel J made the point that a 'good arguable case' imposes a higher merits requirement than the 'serious issue to be tried' test commonly used in applications to amend. Experts' reports supporting the claim, or a body of documentary evidence, might achieve the higher standard. This was a fraud claim. Matters such as a lack of involvement in negotiating the impugned transactions, unconvincing evidence from the defendants to explain their conduct, suspicious phraseology (here, a letter referring to 'the delicate nature of our exchanges'), and attempts to prevent outsiders finding out, could produce a good arguable case.

Worldwide freezing injunction

38.9 *Banco Nacional de Comercio Exterior SNC v Empresa de Telecommunicaciones de Cuba SA* [2007] EWCA Civ 662, LTL 4/7/2007. A post-judgment domestic freezing injunction was granted following the registration under Regulation (EC) No. 44/2001 of a judgment obtained in Turin. The judgment debtor then said it had assigned the debts owed to it to another State-controlled company based in Cuba. On the basis of this information a worldwide freezing injunction was granted. On appeal it was held that there is no jurisdiction under Regulation (EC) No. 44/2001, art. 47, to grant a worldwide freezing injunction. All this provision says is that a person with a judgment which must be recognised is not prevented from applying for protective measures before registration.

A worldwide order would not be made under the Civil Jurisdiction and Judgments Act 1982, s. 25, as it would be inexpedient to do so. The judgment debtor was outside the jurisdiction, the original judgment was granted in Italy, any assets within the jurisdiction were covered by the domestic freezing injunction, and granting a worldwide order would be likely to give rise to disharmony and confusion. It is not the policy of the Italian courts to grant worldwide freezing orders.

Amedeo Hotels Ltd Partnership v Zaman [2007] EWHC 295 (Comm), LTL 14/6/2007. The non-availability of worldwide freezing orders in New York (where the main proceedings were located) was regarded as a reason in favour of granting an English worldwide order, rather than as a reason against doing so.

VARIATION OR DISCHARGE OF A FREEZING INJUNCTION

Discharge on the basis of material non-disclosure

Amedeo Hotels Ltd Partnership v Zaman [2007] EWHC 295 (Comm), LTL 14/6/2007. A past record **38.35** on the part of the defendant of breaking court orders and assisting others to do so for financial gain is a reason for reimposing freezing injunctive relief despite material non-disclosure.

FREEZING INJUNCTIONS AFTER JUDGMENT

Banco Nacional de Comercio Exterior SNC v Empresa de Telecommunicaciones de Cuba SA [2007] EWCA **38.40** Civ 662, LTL 4/7/2007. The Court of Appeal said that the giving of judgment was unlikely to affect any loss caused by third parties from the fact the judgment debtor's assets have been frozen. Therefore, it was held that a domestic freezing injunction granted after registration of a foreign judgment should be varied to include such an undertaking.

Earlier cases indicating that such an undertaking is not required in post-judgment freezing injunctions are therefore to be treated as overruled. Whether this is good practice is another matter. The reason why such undertakings are not insisted upon after judgment is that the risk of the injunction being discharged is minimal, as the claimant has already won. A claimant who has obtained a pre-judgment freezing injunction has only shown a good arguable case, but there is a substantial risk that the claim will not succeed at trial.

Chapter 42   Case Management

TIME WHEN TRACK ALLOCATION IS DECIDED

Point (g). Old PD 49B has been replaced by PD 49, which does not expressly refer to track **42.6** allocation. However, most proceedings to which PD 49 applies must be commenced by Part 8 claim form (PD 49, para. 5), and so are allocated to the multi-track by CPR, r. 8.9(c).

ALLOCATION QUESTIONNAIRES

Cases where allocation questionnaires are not used

42.8 Old PD 49B has been replaced by PD 49, which does not expressly refer to track allocation (see update to 42.6).

Allocation fees and non-payment

42.12 As from 1 October 2007, the allocation fee is £35 if the case is on the small claims track and the claim exceeds £1,500, or £200 if the case is on the fast track or the multi-track (CPFO, fee 2.1). Rules on remission of fees are now in CPFO, sch. 1A.

Chapter 44   Fast Track

LISTING QUESTIONNAIRES: PRE-TRIAL CHECKLISTS

44.10 CPFO, fee 2.2, is now £100, but a new fast track hearing fee of £500 (fee 2.3) is payable at the same time. There is no longer a refund of fee 2.2, but a percentage of fee 2.3 will be refunded by the court on receipt of written notice from the payer of the fee that the case has been settled or discontinued. The percentage refund is 100 per cent if the court is notified more than 28 days before the hearing; 75 per cent if notified between 14 and 28 days before the hearing; 50 per cent if notified between seven and 14 days before the hearing (CPFO, notes following fee 2.3).

Chapter 45   Multi-track

LISTING QUESTIONNAIRES: PRE-TRIAL CHECKLISTS

45.16 CPFO, fee 2.2, is now £100, but a new multi-track hearing fee of £1,000 (fee 2.3) is payable at the same time. There is no longer a refund of fee 2.2, but a percentage of fee 2.3 will be refunded by the court on receipt of written notice from the payer of the fee that the case has been settled or discontinued. The percentage refund is 100 per cent if the court is notified more than 28 days before the hearing; 75 per cent if notified between 14 and 28 days before the hearing; 50 per cent if notified between seven and 14 days before the hearing (CPFO, notes following fee 2.3).

Chapter 46   Non-compliance, Sanctions and Relief

Unless orders

46.10 *Lexi Holdings plc v Luqman* (2007) LTL 7/8/2007. Where an unless order is sought against a party as a sanction for failure to comply with an order, but the party provides written evidence that it has complied, the court may reject that evidence if it finds it is incredible. There is no higher standard, such as 'plainly incredible'. If the evidence is rejected, it is almost inevitable that an unless order will be made.

EXTENSIONS OF TIME

Applying to extend time

Keen Phillips v Field [2006] EWCA Civ 1524, [2007] 1 WLR 686. The court has power to extend time **46.21** on its own initiative under CPR, rr. 3.1(2)(a) and 3.3, even where the extension relates to an unless order.

NON-COMPLIANCE WITH ORDER IMPOSING A SANCTION

Jani-King (GB) Ltd v Prodger [2007] EWHC 712 (QB), LTL 10/4/2007. The test on expiry of an unless **46.29** order is whether there has been complete compliance with the terms of the order, subject only to *de minimis* exceptions (*Hytec Information Systems Ltd v Coventry City Council* [1997] 1 WLR 1666).

Marcan Shipping (London) Ltd v Kefalas [2007] EWCA Civ 463, [2007] 1 WLR 1864. The sanction embodied in an 'unless' order takes effect without the need for any further order if there is a material failure to comply. If the innocent party applies for judgment under CPR, r. 3.5, the court's function is limited to deciding what order should properly be made to reflect the sanction which has already taken effect.

RELIEF FROM SANCTIONS

Principles governing applications for relief

Keen Phillips v Field [2006] EWCA Civ 1524, [2007] 1 WLR 686. The court has power to grant relief **46.31** from a sanction without an application by the party in default by making an order on its own initiative extending time under CPR, rr. 3.1(2)(a) and 3.3.

Jani-King (GB) Ltd v Prodger [2007] EWHC 712 (QB), LTL 10/4/2007. Relief may be granted on terms that the defaulting party fully complies with the terms of the relevant order.

Chapter 48   Disclosure

REFUSAL TO DISCLOSE OR PERMIT INSPECTION

Atos Consulting Ltd v Avis plc [2007] EWHC 323 (TCC), LTL 5/7/2007. On an application under **48.23** CPR, r. 31.19(5), on a disputed claim to withhold inspection, the correct procedure is:

(a) to consider the evidence produced on the application;
(b) to uphold the right to withhold inspection if this is established on the evidence and no sufficient grounds are put forward for challenging that right;
(c) to order inspection if the evidence does not establish a right to withhold the documents;
(d) to order further evidence to be produced if insufficient grounds have been shown for challenging the alleged right to withhold, or for the court to inspect the documents if there is no other means of deciding the matter; and
(e) to invite representations after any inspection.

On the facts, redacted parts of certain board minutes were irrelevant as they did not relate to the project in issue or related matters, so no inspection was ordered for these documents. Redacted parts of certain reports were alleged to contain privileged material, but the reports had been compiled by employees rather than lawyers, so there were sufficient grounds in the challenge to justify inspection.

PRIVILEGE AGAINST SELF-INCRIMINATION

Common law rule

48.38 The precise scope of the privilege against self-incrimination has been modified as a result of the introduction into United Kingdom law of the European Convention on Human Rights by the Human Rights Act 1998.

C plc v P (Attorney-General intervening) [2007] EWCA Civ 493, [2007] 3 WLR 437. When a search order was being executed the defendant asserted his privilege against self-incrimination, and subject to that allowed his computers to be delivered to the supervising solicitor. Highly objectionable images were found on the computers. The claimant applied for directions on what it should do with the images. The judge ordered that they be handed to the police. At first instance the judge held:

(a) In civil cases, before the Human Rights Act 1998, the privilege applied to incriminating answers to questions, documents and articles (*Rank Film Distributors Ltd v Video Information Centre* [1982] AC 380). So the privilege applied to the images.

(b) The effect of the Human Rights Act 1998 is that the privilege does not apply in criminal cases in relation to 'independent evidence'. This is evidence that exists independently of any compulsory questioning or compulsory court process.

(c) The court can adjust the civil scope of the privilege so that it corresponds with the criminal position.

All three members of the Court of Appeal allowed the disclosure of the evidence to the prosecuting authorities. The minority judgment (Lawrence Collins LJ) did so on the wording of the original order. The majority allowed disclosure on the basis that after the Human Rights Act 1998 there is no difference between civil and criminal cases, so the privilege does not apply to free-standing evidence (notwithstanding *Rank Film Distribution Ltd v Video Information Centre*).

Statutory limitations on the rule

48.39 *Kensington International Ltd v Congo* [2007] EWHC 1632 (Comm), LTL 24/7/2007. The claimant had obtained judgment against the Republic of Congo, but was experiencing difficulty in obtaining payment. It sought *Norwich Pharmacal* orders against a company and an individual who had been engaged in oil trading with the Republic, seeking information and documents on the Republic's assets. It was alleged that these persons were more than merely 'mixed up' in the wrongdoing, but had been involved in bribery and other conduct which, if proved, would be criminal offences under UK law. The respondents objected to providing the information and documents relying on the privilege against self-incrimination.

If the *Norwich Pharmacal* application was to be considered in isolation, it was not a form of 'proceedings relating to property' as required by the Fraud Act 2006, s. 13. However, the correct view was to treat the *Norwich Pharmacal* application as ancillary to the ongoing attempts to enforce the judgment debt, which was a proceeding seeking the recovery of property. The corruption offences identified by the respondents were not offences under the Fraud Act 2006, but they were covered by the partial removal of the privilege in s. 13 because they were 'related offences' for the purposes of that section, involving 'fraudulent conduct or purpose'. Disclosure was ordered.

LEGAL PROFESSIONAL PRIVILEGE

Communications connected to litigation

Stax Claimants v Bank of Nova Scotia Channel Islands Ltd [2007] EWHC 1153 (Ch), LTL 23/5/2007. A **48.47** meeting between lawyers on opposing sides who might have common interests (here the lawyers represented claimants and third parties) to discuss 'battle tactics' in the litigation was not covered by without-prejudice privilege. The discussion, or parts of it, might well be protected by legal professional privilege. Views expressed at such a meeting on the strengths and weaknesses of the parties' claims and defences, and discussion of tactics in the litigation, are likely to be protected by legal professional privilege. Discussions on disclosure were regarded as difficult, because the documents may or may not have been confidential. Discussion of case management issues and the administration of the litigation are not disclosable at all.

WITHOUT-PREJUDICE COMMUNICATIONS

Framlington Group Ltd v Barnetson [2007] EWCA Civ 502, [2007] IRLR 598. Without-prejudice **48.54** privilege applies to genuine attempts to negotiate a settlement of a dispute where the parties contemplate or might reasonably have contemplated litigation if they cannot agree. The question of proximity applies to the subject matter of the dispute, rather than the length of time before the threat or actual commencement of the contemplated litigation.

Stax Claimants v Bank of Nova Scotia Channel Islands Ltd [2007] EWHC 1153 (Ch), LTL 23/5/2007. A meeting between lawyers on opposing sides who might have common interests (here the lawyers represented claimants and third parties), which was not for the purpose of negotiating settlement, but rather to discuss 'battle tactics' in the litigation, was not covered by without-prejudice privilege. Parts of it might well be protected by legal professional privilege.

Proof of settlement

Jackson v Thakrar [2007] EWHC 271 (TCC), LTL 7/3/2007. In this case a chain of letters came into **48.55** being without an intention to create legal relations, and at best amounted to an agreement to agree on a single topic. No settlement had been reached.

Brown v Rice [2007] EWHC 625 (Ch), [2007] CILL 2467. An offer made in mediation did not deal with how the litigation should be disposed of, and had not been made in writing as previously stipulated. It was therefore incomplete, and there was no final settlement.

WAIVER OF PRIVILEGE

Compagnie Noga d'Importation et d'Exportation SA v Australia and New Zealand Banking Group Ltd **48.59** [2007] EWHC 85 (Comm), LTL 5/2/2007. The defendant had made five affidavits, with the assistance of solicitors, about his assets pursuant to clauses in a freezing injunction. As a result he had waived any claim to privilege on the issue of disclosure of his assets.

PRE-ACTION DISCLOSURE

Requirements for pre-action disclosure

Total E & P Soudan SA v Edmonds [2007] EWCA Civ 50, LTL 31/1/2007. Generally, the court should **48.71** not embark on an investigation into issues such as justiciability or the elements of the alleged cause of action, on an application for pre-action disclosure. These matters can be left until after proceedings are issued. It is different if the respondent can show beyond argument that a claim is hopeless or non-justiciable.

Discretion to order pre-action disclosure

48.72 *Total E & P Soudan SA v Edmonds* [2007] EWCA Civ 50, LTL 31/1/2007. This was a complex claim, and one of the reasons for exercising the discretion in favour of pre-action disclosure was the desirability of having a focused pleading from the outset.

Costs of pre-action disclosure applications

48.75 *SES Contracting Ltd v UK Coal plc* [2007] EWCA Civ 791, LTL 26/7/2007. The starting point on costs is that the applicant must pay the respondent's costs of an application for pre-action disclosure (CPR, r. 48.1). This implicitly recognises that it is not usually unreasonable for a respondent to resist such an application. It might be right to depart from the normal rule if the application were resisted in an unreasonable way, such as by using written evidence not backed up by contemporaneous documents.

NORWICH PHARMACAL ORDERS

48.83 *Nikitin v Richards Butler* [2007] EWHC 173 (QB), LTL 19/2/2007. A *Norwich Pharmacal* order was refused where proceedings could fairly be brought without further disclosure, and where the order only served to increase the overall costs.

Mersey Care NHS Trust v Ackroyd [2007] EWCA Civ 101, [2007] HRLR 19. A *Norwich Pharmacal* order was refused as against a journalist despite an earlier order against his newspaper that it disclose the identity of its journalist involved in the same leak. The facts were different from the earlier application, and it was not necessary or proportionate to make the order.

Campaign Against Arms Trade v BAE Systems plc [2007] EWHC 330 (QB), LTL 6/3/2007. A *Norwich Pharmacal* order was made to identify the source of a leaked email, where the defendant had supplied a redacted version of the leaked email to the claimant with all information which could have assisted in identifying the source of the leak removed.

Chapter 56   Giving Evidence without Attending Court

LETTERS OF REQUEST FROM FOREIGN COURTS

Injunction restraining deposing witness

56.15 *Benfield Holdings Ltd v Richardson* [2007] EWHC 171 (QB), LTL 1/3/2007. An injunction may be granted to restrain a party from deposing a witness for the purpose of foreign proceedings. The basis of the jurisdiction to do so is unconscionable conduct. It may be unconscionable where the pursuit of foreign proceedings is vexatious or oppressive or interferes with the due process of the court.

Chapter 59   Trial

SETTLEMENT BEFORE TRIAL

The listing fee is no longer refunded but a percentage of the hearing fee (fee 2.3) will be **59.15** refunded by the court on receipt of written notice from the payer of the fee that the case has been settled or discontinued. The percentage refund is 100 per cent if the court is notified more than 28 days before the hearing; 75 per cent if notified between 14 and 28 days before the hearing; 50 per cent if notified between seven and 14 days before the hearing (CPFO, notes following fee 2.3).

PRE-TRIAL ARRANGEMENTS

Hearings in public and in private

A. F. Noonan (Architectural Practice) Ltd v Bournemouth and Boscombe Athletic Community Football **59.20** *Club Ltd* [2007] EWCA Civ 848, *The Times*, 12 July 2007. An order for a hearing to take place in private under CPR, r. 39.2(3), does not render all information in the proceedings secret. Giving an interview to the press about details in such a hearing will not be a contempt of court unless there is also an express order prohibiting publication of such information under the Administration of Justice Act 1960, s. 12(1)(e).

Impartiality of judge

Application of the informed observer test   *Steadman-Byrne v Amjad* [2007] EWCA Civ 625, *The* **59.28** *Times*, 30 July 2007. It is unacceptable for a judge to form, or to give the impression of having formed, a firm view on the credibility of the evidence of one side before the other side has called any evidence. Such conduct would give rise to a real possibility of bias in the mind of a fair-minded observer.

CONDUCT OF THE TRIAL

Summary disposal of issues at the start of a trial

Western Broadcasting Services v Seaga [2007] UKPC 19, LTL 3/4/2007. There is a list of case **59.35** management powers in CPR, r. 3.1(2), and by r. 1.4(2)(c) active case management includes disposing of issues summarily. These powers were assumed to be wide enough to encompass deciding an issue on whether settlement negotiations had resulted in a binding agreement in a summary fashion. However, given that a final decision was being made, doing so on the basis of written evidence alone was held to be unfair and outside the ambit of these powers, and the witnesses should have been called for cross-examination.

Chapter 61   Judgments and Orders

EMBARGOED JUDGMENTS

Crown Prosecution Service v P [2007] EWHC 1144 (Admin), LTL 6/6/2007. Disclosure of a judgment **61.30** under PD 40E was for the purpose of the direct legal team taking instructions for the immediate conduct of the case. This means that while it was appropriate for junior solicitors to consult with their immediate supervising solicitor (and vice versa), wider circulation was impermissible.

REVIEW OF JUDGMENT

Slip rule

61.37 *R+V Versicherung AG v Risk Insurance and Reinsurance Solutions SA* [2007] EWHC 79 (Comm), *The Times*, 26 February 2007. The slip rule in CPR, r. 40.12(1), cannot be used to correct matters of substance. The appropriate avenue for such matters is to appeal.

Swindale v Forder [2007] EWCA Civ 29, [2007] 1 FLR 1905. The slip rule can be used for the purpose of giving effect to the intention of the court.

Chapter 62   Interest

RATE OF INTEREST

62.14 *McGlinn v Waltham Contractors Ltd* [2007] EWHC 698 (TCC), LTL 11/4/2007. Interest at 1 per cent above base rate was awarded against a builder in respect of defective building work.

PERIOD OF INTEREST

62.16 *McGlinn v Waltham Contractors Ltd* [2007] EWHC 698 (TCC), LTL 11/4/2007. Interest was awarded from the date of issue of proceedings against a builder in respect of defective building work.

Chapter 63   Solicitor and Own Client Costs

CONTENTIOUS BUSINESS AGREEMENTS

63.11 *Re Wilson Properties UK Ltd, Wilson v The Specter Partnership* [2007] EWHC 133 (Ch), LTL 9/2/2007. An agreement will be a contentious business agreement if it satisfies the requirements of the Solicitors Act 1974, s. 59. There is no need for it to be expressly stated to be a 'contentious business agreement'.

Chapter 64   Part 36 Offers

NON-DISCLOSURE

Split trials and Part 36 offers

64.6 *Shepherds Investments Ltd v Walters* [2007] EWCA Civ 292, LTL 3/4/2007. The Court of Appeal upheld the trial judge's decision to reserve costs until the outcome of an account for profits in a case where there was a claimant's Part 36 offer. This case goes further than *HSS Hire Services Group plc v BMB Builders Merchants Ltd* [2005] EWCA Civ 626, [2005] 1 WLR 3158, where the offer had been made by the losing defendant, rather than the winning claimant. It emphasises the breadth of the judge's discretion on the form of costs orders available after a split trial.

ACCEPTANCE

Costs consequences of accepting a Part 36 offer

Acceptance of Part 36 offers after the relevant period   *Matthews v Metal Improvements Co. Inc.* [2007] EWCA Civ 215, LTL 14/3/2007. On the question of costs after receipt of a Part 36 offer for which permission was given for acceptance after the 21-day period, the judge had asked whether it had been reasonable for the claimant not to have accepted the offer when it was made. The Court of Appeal said this was a fundamental misunderstanding of the function of a Part 36 offer, which is to put the claimant on risk as to costs if, as a result of the contingencies of litigation, it later transpired that the claimant was unable to beat the terms of the offer. On the facts, the value of the claim diminished after the offer was made, because of a medical condition which was unrelated to the accident. That provided no basis for departing from the usual rule that the claimant should pay the defendant's costs from the expiry of the 21-day period if the offer was accepted late.   **64.27**

Other consequences of acceptance

Enforcement of agreed terms   *Orton v Collins* [2007] EWHC 803 (Ch), [2007] 3 All ER 863. Where the terms of the acceptance include the disposition of an interest in land, the court has the power to order the parties to sign a single document incorporating the terms of the settlement.   **64.35**

Chapter 65   Security for Costs

THE RESPONDENT

Claimants

Newman v Wenden Properties Ltd [2007] EWHC 336 (TCC), LTL 24/4/2007. Where a counterclaim is an entirely separate cross-claim, with an independent validity of its own, it is treated as a separate claim for the purposes of ordering security for costs (*Hutchison Telephone (UK) Ltd v Ultimate Response Ltd* [1993] BCLC 307).   **65.3**

EXERCISE OF THE COURT'S DISCRETION

Stifling a genuine claim

Kuenyehia v International Hospitals Group Limited [2007] EWCA Civ 274, LTL 27/2/2007. The claimant has the burden of satisfying the court that ordering security for costs will stifle a genuine claim, if that is the claimant's assertion. The claimant produced misleading documentation and made inconsistent statements about the assets available for funding the claim, so the court made an order for security for costs.   **65.19**

Newman v Wenden Properties Ltd [2007] EWHC 336 (TCC), LTL 24/4/2007. It is for the party resisting security to show how and why other sources of funding are not available to fund the claim.

Chapter 66   Costs Orders

GENERAL PRINCIPLES

Discretion on costs

66.5   *Straker v Tudor Rose* [2007] EWCA Civ 368, LTL 25/4/2007. The defendant solicitors acted for both sides in a proposed transaction to purchase two properties off-plan, conditional on obtaining finance by a particular date. The claimant sued the solicitors for failing to seek an extension to that date when the finance was not available in time. The solicitors made a Part 36 offer to the effect that the claimant would in any event only have obtained finance for one of the properties. At trial the claimant won in respect of only the one property, but recovered damages exceeding the amount offered by the solicitors. The judge awarded the claimant only limited pre-action costs, and no costs from issue, on the ground that the claimant had failed to negotiate, on the theory that if he had done so the defendant would have improved the offer above the amount awarded at trial. This was held to be so seriously wrong that it was outside the generous ambit of the discretion on costs. Partial success on the claim justified a one-third or one-quarter reduction in the claimant's costs. Adding a proportionate further discount for non-compliance with the protocol (not negotiating), the Court of Appeal substituted an overall award of 60 per cent of the claimant's post-issue costs.

Charles Church Developments Ltd v Stent Foundations Ltd [2007] EWHC 855 (TCC), [2007] CILL 2477. Costs consequences of non-compliance with pre-action protocols should generally be dealt with at an early stage.

Partial success

66.11   **Partial success to be taken into account**   *Actavis Ltd v Merck and Co. Inc.* [2007] EWHC 1625 (Pat), LTL 7/8/2007. The starting point on final costs orders is that the winner should be awarded the whole of its costs of the proceedings, even if there were issues on which he had been unsuccessful. However, depriving the winner of a percentage of his costs did not rest on a need to find unreasonable or improper conduct. In practical terms, the courts are quite ready to find exceptions to the general rule, particularly in cases of partial success where there is no significant overlap between the issues on which the respective parties were successful.

National Westminster Bank plc v Kotonou [2007] EWCA Civ 223, LTL 26/2/2007. The claimant sought to have a guarantee set aside on five grounds, four of which were unsuccessful. The Court of Appeal held that the case called for a percentage costs order, and said it would have been a surprise if the judge had awarded the claimant the whole of his costs. The claimant was awarded 50 per cent of his costs.

MULTIPLE PARTIES AND CLAIMS

Bullock and *Sanderson* orders

66.42   *McGlinn v Waltham Contractors Ltd* [2007] EWHC 698 (TCC), LTL 11/4/2007. A *Bullock* order was refused in a building case. While these orders have been preserved by CPR, r. 44.3, the fact certain of the pleaded claims had failed against both defendants meant such an order was inappropriate.

BEDDOE ORDERS

66.51   CPR, r. 19.9(7), is now r. 19.9E. The fact that a pre-emptive costs order is sought when making a derivative claim must be stated in the claim form (PD 19C, para. 2(2)). If indemnity is also sought for the costs of the application for permission to continue the claim, that must be stated in the permission application (PD 19C, para. 2(2)).

Protective costs orders

R (Bullmore) v West Hertfordshire Hospitals NHS Trust [2007] EWCA Civ 609, LTL 27/6/2007. A **66.52** protective costs order was refused on the ground that the case was not sufficiently exceptional.

COSTS LIMITATION ORDERS

Willis v Nicolson [2007] EWCA Civ 199, [2007] PIQR P22. It is for the Civil Procedure Rule **66.53** Committee to lay down principles on when costs capping orders should be made.

PUBLICLY FUNDED LITIGANTS

Procedure in applications against the Legal Services Commission

In the LSC, the title 'regional director' has been changed to 'director'. **66.61**

NON-PARTY COSTS ORDERS

Costs orders against experts

Admiral Insurance Services Ltd v Daniels (Cambridge County Court 2007) LTL 14/6/2007). An expert **66.68** was rendered jointly and severally liable with the losing party for the costs of the claim on the ground that he had produced a damage assessment report without having examined the vehicle in question.

Chapter 67   Fixed and Predictable Costs on Judgments etc.

FIXED PERCENTAGE INCREASE IN ROAD TRAFFIC ACCIDENT CLAIMS

Lamont v Burton [2007] EWCA Civ 429, [2007] 3 All ER 173. The claimant in a road traffic accident **67.16** case funded under a CFA failed to beat a Part 36 offer at trial. It was held that the 100 per cent uplift applied as the case had been concluded at trial. CPR, Part 44, could not be used to circumvent the clear wording of r. 45.16 so as to give the court a discretion which was not stated in Part 45.

Chapter 68   Assessment of Costs

FAST TRACK TRIAL COSTS

Fixed trial costs

The fixed trial costs for fast track claims had remained unchanged since 1998, and had fallen **68.6** behind the rate of inflation. This has been rectified from 1 October 2007, with the Civil

Procedure (Amendment) Rules 2007 (SI 2007/2204), r. 22, providing that the new rates apply where the hearing of a fast track trial commences on or after 1 October 2007. The old rates apply to trials starting before 1 October 2007. The new rates set out in CPR, rr. 46.2 and 46.3, are:

Advocate's fees for preparing for and attending trial

Value of the claim	Amount of fast track costs which the court may award
No more than £3,000	£485
More than £3,000 but not more than £10,000	£690
More than £10,000	£1,035

Legal representative attending to assist the advocate

Where this fee is permitted by r. 46.3(2), it is raised from £250 to £345.

Additional amount on the separate trial of an issue

Where this additional amount is permitted, it is raised from £350 to £485.

DETAILED ASSESSMENT

68.9 *Lahey v Pirelli Tyres Ltd* [2007] EWCA Civ 91, [2007] 1 WLR 998. A costs judge does not have jurisdiction to make a percentage reduction in the costs payable before starting a detailed assessment.

Appeals against assessment decisions

68.28 The time limit for bringing an appeal from an authorised court officer in detailed assessment proceedings is changed from 14 to 21 days as from 1 October 2007 (Civil Procedure (Amendment) Rules 2007 (SI 2007/2204), r. 15(b)). This brings this type of appeal into line with other civil appeals, which also have a 21-day time limit.

Chapter 71   The Appeals System

ROUTES OF APPEAL

Final decisions in specialist and multi-track claims

71.4 **Kinds of claims and proceedings in which final appeals are to the Court of Appeal**   Old PD 49B has been replaced by PD 49, which does not expressly refer to track allocation. However, most proceedings to which PD 49 applies must be commenced by Part 8 claim form (PD 49, para. 5), and so are allocated to the multi-track by CPR, r. 8.9(c).

Transfer of appeals to the Court of Appeal

71.9 *7E Communications Ltd v Vertex Antennentechnik GmbH* [2007] EWCA Civ 140, [2007] 1 CLC 417. CPR, r. 52.14, allows a lower court or an appeal court to order an appeal to be transferred to the Court of Appeal if the appeal will raise an important point of principle or if there is some other compelling reason for doing so. An order under r. 52.14 cannot be made by a judge of a lower court who refuses permission to appeal, because, until permission to appeal is granted, there is no appeal to be transferred.

TIME FOR APPEALING

Time limits

The time limit for bringing an appeal from an authorised court officer in detailed assessment proceedings is changed from 14 to 21 days as from 1 October 2007 (Civil Procedure (Amendment) Rules 2007 (SI 2007/2204), r. 15(b)). This brings this type of appeal into line with other civil appeals, which also have a 21-day time limit. **71.19**

STRIKING OUT OR IMPOSING CONDITIONS

Sanctions and conditions in appeals

Masri v Consolidated Contractors International (UK) Ltd [2007] EWCA Civ 702, LTL 31/7/2007. A **71.45** condition was imposed requiring payment of an interim payment and costs ordered in the court below, with a sanction of striking out the appeal in the event of default.

STATUTORY APPEALS

With effect from 1 October 2007, the new CPR, r. 52.12A, provides that in a statutory **71.53** appeal any person may apply for permission to file evidence or make representations in the appeal. Such an application must be made promptly (r. 52.12A(2)).

There are new rr. 52.18 to 52.20 dealing with statutory appeals under the Law of Property Act 1922, appeals from certain tribunals, and appeals under certain planning legislation.

Provisions in RSC, ord. 93, rr. 4, 5, 9, 10, 16, 17, 18 and 19; ord. 94, rr. 4, 5, 8, 9, 12 and 13; ord. 95, rr. 1, 4, 5 and 6; and CCR, ord. 45, are revoked with effect from 1 October 2007.

Chapter 72   Hearing of Appeals

REVIEW OF THE DECISION BELOW

Review not rehearing

McFaddens Solicitors v Chandrasekaran [2007] EWCA Civ 220, LTL 26/2/2007. In this appeal against a **72.5** summary judgment decision, the appeal court could only have fulfilled its task by reference to all the material put before the master. While this looks like a rehearing, it was to be regarded as a review within the meaning of CPR, r. 52.11.

Chapter 73   Appeals to the House of Lords

LEAPFROG APPEALS

R (Jones) v Ceredigion County Council [2007] UKHL 24, [2007] 1 WLR 1400. An appellant with two **73.3** grounds of appeal was given permission to use the leapfrog procedure on only one ground. The permission to use the leapfrog procedure is couched in terms of a proposal. If taken up, the appellant is limited to the terms of the proposal, and will have to abandon the other ground. If refused, the appellant is able (with the appropriate permission) to take both grounds to the Court of Appeal. What is to be avoided is allowing a party to bring appeals in parallel to both the Court of Appeal and the House of Lords on different issues arising from the same order.

Chapter 79   Winding Up and Administration of Registered Companies

PROCEEDINGS ON CONTRIBUTORY'S PETITION

Procedure on a contributory's petition

79.67 **Presentation of a petition**   Old PD 49B, para. 9(2) to (7), has been replaced by new PD 49B, paras 2 to 7.

Chapter 81   Insolvency Applications and Appeals

APPLICATIONS IN INSOLVENCY PROCEEDINGS

Originating and ordinary applications

81.2 Where there are two joined matters between the same parties, one of which is an insolvency application and the other requires a different form of originating process, both may be commenced by the insolvency application (CPR, r. 7.3; *Re Prestige Grindings Ltd* [2005] EWHC 3076 (Ch), [2006] 1 BCLC 440).

LITIGATION AGAINST PERSONS SUBJECT TO INSOLVENCY PROCEEDINGS

Retrospective permission

81.33 In *Seal v Chief Constable of South Wales Police* [2007] UKHL 31, [2007] 1 WLR 1910, Lord Bingham of Cornhill said, at [7], that he did not think that the question whether proceedings commenced without permission are void:

should ordinarily turn on a detailed consideration of the language used by Parliament in one provision as compared with that used in another. The important question is whether, in requiring a particular condition to be satisfied before proceedings are brought, Parliament intended to confer a substantial protection on the putative defendant, such as to invalidate proceedings brought without meeting the condition, or to impose a procedural requirement giving rights to the defendant if a claimant should fail to comply with the requirement; but not nullifying the proceedings: see *R v Soneji* [2005] UKHL 49, [2006] 1 AC 340, at [23].

In *Seal v Chief Constable of South Wales Police* a majority of the House of Lords held that retrospective leave could not be given to bring civil proceedings in respect of an act purporting to be done in pursuance of the Mental Health Act 1983, as required by s. 139(2) of that Act. However, this does not overrule decisions that retrospective leave could be given under similar provisions in other legislation. In particular, *Re Saunders* [1997] Ch 60, in which it was held that retrospective leave could be given for proceedings against a bankrupt, and which was mentioned by Lord Bingham at [6], was not overruled.

In *Godfrey v Torpy* [2007] Bus LR 1203 the learned deputy judge said that he preferred, and would if necessary have applied, *Re Saunders* [1997] Ch 60 (retrospective permission may be given) rather than *Re Taylor* [2006] EWHC 3029 (Ch), [2007] Ch 150 (retrospective permission cannot be given). Such disagreement amongst first-instance judges is highly undesirable. In principle, where a first-instance judge is faced with a point on which there are two previous inconsistent decisions from judges of coordinate jurisdiction, the second of those decisions should be followed in the absence of cogent reasons to the contrary (*Colchester Estates (Cardiff) v Carlton Industries plc* [1986] Ch 80 at pp. 84–85 per Nourse J). In *Re Taylor*, at [46], Judge Kershaw QC, justifying his refusal to follow *Re Saunders*, said that this was not a correct principle. But the principle was subsequently affirmed by Neuberger LJ in *Re Lune Metal Products Ltd* [2006] EWCA Civ 1720, [2007] Bus LR 589, at [9].

Chapter 82   Applications under the Companies Act 1985

INTRODUCTION

Jurisdiction to hear applications under the Companies Act 1985

The provisions of the Companies Act 2006 relating to registration of companies will come into force on 1 October 2008, but some other provisions are being brought into force before then.   **82.1**

Purpose of applications under the Companies Act 1985

Sections 459 to 461 of the Companies Act 1985 have been replaced by ss. 994 to 999 of the   **82.2** Companies Act 2006 as from 1 October 2007. Sections 425 to 427 of the Companies Act 1985 will be replaced by ss. 895 to 901 of the Companies Act 2006 on 6 April 2008. The Companies Act 1985, s. 216, was replaced by the Companies Act 2006, s. 794, on 20 January 2007.

Procedural rules on litigation concerning the affairs of companies

Old PD 49B has been replaced by PD 49, which applies to applications under the Companies   **82.3** Act 2006 as well as those under the Companies Act 1985 and related legislation. PD 49 does not apply to derivative claims (PD 49, para. 2(b); see the update note to 14.42). Unlike old PD 49B, the new PD 49 does not require any applications to be brought by petition. However, applications in respect of unfairly prejudicial conduct of a company's affairs are still required by statute to be brought by petition (Companies Act 2006, s. 994(1), replacing the Companies Act 1985, s. 459(1)).

Old PD 49B, para. 2(1), is now PD 49, para. 2. PD 49 is applied to proceedings relating to limited liability partnerships by para. 3. Old PD 49B, para. 3B, is now PD 49, paras 16 and 17. Old PD 49B, para. 14, is now PD 49, para. 18. Paragraphs 3A, 3B(1)(a) and 14(2) of old PD 49B have not been reproduced in PD 49.

PROCEDURE FOR MAKING AN APPLICATION

Commencement by petition

Old PD 49B has been replaced by PD 49, which no longer requires any applications to be   **82.4** commenced by petition.

Commencement by Part 8 claim form

82.5 Old PD 49B has been replaced by PD 49. This requires all applications to which it applies to be commenced by Part 8 claim form (PD 49, para. 5(1)), except for the following, which must be commenced by Part 7 claim form:

    (a) an application under the Companies Act 2006, s. 169 (for an order relieving a company from its obligation to notify members of a director's representations concerning a resolution to remove him from office) (PD 49, para. 10);

    (b) an application under the Companies Act 2006, s. 295 (for an order relieving a private company from its obligation to circulate a members' statement concerning a resolution which they are proposing) (PD 49, para. 11);

    (c) an application under the Companies Act 2006, s. 317 (for an order relieving a company from its obligation to circulate a member's statement concerning business of a general meeting) (PD 49, para. 11);

    (d) an application under the Companies Act 2006, s. 370 (claim by members of a company in its name for a remedy for breach of the provisions requiring members' approval of political donations and expenditure) (PD 49, para. 12);

    (e) an application under the Companies Act 2006, s. 955 (for an order to secure compliance with the City Code or with a requirement under s. 947 to disclose documents or information to the Panel on Takeovers and Mergers) (PD 49, para. 13);

    (f) an application under the Companies Act 2006, s. 968(6) (for compensation for breach of an agreement which has been invalidated by a takeover bid because the company is opted into the provisions overriding takeover barriers) (PD 49, para. 14).

Old PD 49B, para. 2(3), is now PD 49, para. 5(2).

Title of proceedings

82.6 Old PD 49B, para. 1(3), is now PD 49, para. 4(1). If the name of a company is changed during the course of proceedings in relation to it, the title of the proceedings must be altered by substituting the new name for the old and adding the old name in brackets at the end of the title (PD 49, para. 4(2)).

Company should be a party to the proceedings

82.6A If the company concerned is not the claimant in a claim under the Companies Act 2006, it should be made a defendant to the claim, unless the court orders otherwise (PD 49, para. 9(1)). Where an application is made under the Companies Act 2006 in proceedings to which the company concerned is, or is required to be, a defendant, the company must be made a respondent to the application unless the court orders otherwise (PD 49, para. 9(2)).

A claim commenced by the company concerned need not have a defendant if it is under the Companies Act 1985, part 13 (arrangements and reconstructions) (PD 49, para. 7(2)), or under Regulation (EC) No. 2157/2001, art. 26 (PD 49, para. 17(2)).

Service

82.7 Old PD 49B, para. 11, has been replaced by PD 49, para. 20. Neither the High Court nor a county court will serve documents in companies matters. An application under the Companies Act 1985, s. 721, or the Companies Act 2006, s. 1132 (production and inspection of books where offence suspected), may be made without notice to, or service of the claim form on, any person against whom an order is sought (PD 49, paras 6 and 15).

A copy of a claim form applying for an order under the Companies Act 2006, s. 169, s. 295 or s. 317, must be served on the company (if it is not the claimant) and on the person who required circulation of the statement objected to. If service is not reasonably practicable in the circumstances, the claimant must provide evidence that those persons have been notified of the application (PD 49, paras 10 and 11).

Track allocation

Old PD 49B has been replaced by PD 49, which does not expressly refer to track allocation. **82.8**
However, most proceedings to which PD 49 applies must be commenced by Part 8 claim
form (PD 49, para. 5), and so are allocated to the multi-track by CPR, r. 8.9(c).

UNFAIR PREJUDICE

Statutory provision

As from 1 October 2007, the Companies Act 1985, s. 459, has been replaced by the **82.9**
Companies Act 2006, s. 994.

Procedural rules

As from 1 October 2007, the Companies Act 1985, s. 459, has been replaced by **82.10**
the Companies Act 2006, s. 994. Old PD 49B, para. 9(1), is now new PD 49B, para. 1.

Form and contents of petition

As from 1 October 2007, the Companies Act 1985, s. 459, has been replaced by the **82.11**
Companies Act 2006, s. 994. Old PD 49B, para. 9, is now new PD 49B.

Interim orders

As from 1 October 2007, the Companies Act 1985, s. 459, has been replaced by the **82.15**
Companies Act 2006, s. 994. An application for an order convening a meeting is now made
under the Companies Act 2006, s. 306 (the reference to the Companies Act 1985, s. 317, was
a mistake for s. 371).

Costs

As from 1 October 2007, the Companies Act 1985, s. 459, has been replaced by the **82.16**
Companies Act 2006, s. 994. The Companies Act 1985, s. 309B, has been replaced by
the Companies Act 2006, s. 234.

Court's order

As from 1 October 2007, the Companies Act 1985, s. 461, has been replaced by the **82.17**
Companies Act 2006, s. 996.

Chapter 83   Director Disqualification

MAKING THE APPLICATION

Court to which application is to be made

Under CDDA 1986, s. 6(3)(c), the court to which a disqualification application is to be made **83.5**
where the lead company has been in administration or administrative receivership is the court
which had jurisdiction to wind up the company when the administrator or administrative
receiver was appointed (*Secretary of State for Trade and Industry v Arnold* [2007] EWHC 1933 (Ch),
LTL 16/8/2007). That court has jurisdiction to hear an application even if the company has
been dissolved without going into winding up (ibid.).

FACTORS WHICH THE COURT CONSIDERS IN AN APPLICATION UNDER SECTION 6 OR 8

Evidence

83.21 It is not an abuse of process to allege misconduct that would constitute a criminal offence in director disqualification proceedings where the criminal standard of proof is not required (*Re Mea Corporation Ltd* [2006] EWHC 1846 (Ch), [2007] 1 BCLC 618).

Chapter 90   Homelessness and Housing Act 1996 Appeals

DUTIES AND THEIR DISCHARGE

Provision of interim accommodation

90.36 A decision whether to provide interim accommodation to a claimant pending review of a decision adverse to the claimant may be made by the officer who made the decision which is under review (*R (Shukri Abdi) v Lambeth London Borough Council* [2007] EWHC 1565 (Admin), [2007] NPC 82).

Chapter 93   Anti-social Behaviour and Harassment

HOUSING ACT 1996 INJUNCTIONS

Anti-social behaviour injunction

93.3 As from 6 April 2007, the Housing Act 1996, s. 153A has been replaced by a new s. 153A substituted by the Police and Justice Act 2006, s. 26. This redefines an anti-social behaviour injunction as an injunction that prohibits a person from engaging in housing-related anti-social conduct of a kind specified in the injunction (Housing Act 1996, s. 153A(1)). Conduct prohibited by an anti-social behaviour injunction may be described by reference to a person or persons (s. 153A(4)). If it is, it may be described by reference:

(a) to persons generally;

(b) to persons of a description specified in the injunction; or

(c) to persons, or a person, specified in the injunction.

'Anti-social conduct' means conduct capable of causing nuisance or annoyance to some person (who need not be a particular identified person) (s. 153A(1)). 'Housing-related' means directly or indirectly relating to or affecting the housing management functions of a relevant landlord (s. 153A(1); 'relevant landlord' is defined in s. 153E(7)—see 93.2). 'Conduct' means conduct anywhere (s. 153A(1)).

On the application of a relevant landlord, the court may grant an anti-social behaviour injunction (s. 153A(2)) if the condition in s. 153A(3) is satisfied. That condition is that the person against whom the injunction is sought is engaging, has engaged or threatens to engage in housing-related conduct capable of causing a nuisance or annoyance to:

(a) a person with a right (of whatever description) to reside in or occupy housing accommodation owned or managed by a relevant landlord;

(b) a person with a right (of whatever description) to reside in or occupy other housing accommodation in the neighbourhood of housing accommodation mentioned in paragraph (a);

(c) a person engaged in lawful activity in, or in the neighbourhood of, housing accommodation mentioned in paragraph (a); or

(d) a person employed (whether or not by a relevant landlord) in connection with the exercise of a relevant landlord's housing management functions.

'Housing management functions' include functions conferred by or under any enactment, and the powers and duties of the landlord as the holder of an estate or interest in housing accommodation (s. 153E(11)). 'Housing accommodation' includes flats, lodging-houses and hostels (s. 153E(9)(a)); and the yards, gardens, outhouses and appurtenances belonging to the accommodation and usually enjoyed with it (s. 153E(9)(b)). The 'neighbourhood' of housing accommodation owned or managed by a relevant landlord is said, somewhat circularly, by s. 153E(9)(c), to include the neighbourhood of the whole of the housing accommodation owned or managed by the relevant landlord in the neighbourhood and any common areas used in connection with the accommodation.

POWER OF ARREST ADDED TO LOCAL AUTHORITY'S INJUNCTION

As from 6 April 2007, the Anti-social Behaviour Act 2003, s. 91, is replaced by the Police and Justice Act 2006, s. 27. This has added a power to remand an arrestee, like the power in the Housing Act 1996, s. 155 (see 93.11). **93.12**

If a local authority is a party (by virtue of the Local Government Act 1972, s. 222) to proceedings in which an injunction is granted which prohibits conduct which is capable of causing nuisance or annoyance to a person (the potential victim), the court may attach a power of arrest to any provision of the injunction (Police and Justice Act 2006, s. 27(2)). (The Local Government Act 1972, s. 222, enables a local authority to bring, defend or appear in proceedings for the promotion or protection of the interests of inhabitants of its area.) By the Police and Justice Act 2006, s. 27(2) and (3), the court may attach a power of arrest if it thinks that either:

(a) the conduct being prohibited consists of or includes the use or threatened use of violence; or

(b) there is a significant risk of harm to the potential victim — harm being defined in s. 27(12) as including serious ill-treatment or abuse (whether physical or not).

An application for a power of arrest to be attached to an injunction may be made in the claim form, the acknowledgment of service, the defence or counterclaim in a Part 7 claim, or an application under CPR, Part 23 (r. 65.9(1)). It must be supported by written evidence (r. 65.9(2)). If the application is made on notice, the local authority must serve it, with a copy of the evidence, personally on the person against whom the injunction is sought, not less than two days before the hearing (r. 65.9(3)). Rule 65.4 (notification of police, see 93.9) applies to a power of arrest added under the Police and Justice Act 2006, s. 27 (CPR, r. 65.10(1A)(a)).

Where a power of arrest is added, under the Police and Justice Act 2006, s. 27, to any provision of an injunction obtained by a local authority, a constable may arrest, without warrant, a person whom he has reasonable cause for suspecting to be in breach of that provision (s. 27(4)). After making an arrest, the constable must, as soon as is reasonably practicable, inform the local authority (s. 27(5)). The arrestee must be brought before the court within 24 hours of arrest, excluding Christmas Day, Good Friday or any Sunday (s. 27(6)(a) and (7)). When the arrestee is first brought before a judge, that judge may deal with the matter or adjourn proceedings (CPR, r. 65.6(2) applied by r. 65.10(1A)(b)). If the matter is not disposed of forthwith, the arrestee may be remanded (Police and Justice Act

2006, s. 27(6)(b)), either in custody or on bail, in accordance with sch. 10. The procedure for applying for bail is in CPR, r. 65.7, and PD 65, paras 3.1 to 3.3, as applied by para. 4A.1. There is also a power under the Police and Justice Act 2006, s. 27(9), (10) and (11), to remand for a medical report or a report on mental condition (see PD 65, paras 4.1 and 4A.2). Paragraphs (4) and (5) of CPR, r. 65.6 (time limit on dealing with an arrestee who is released, see 93.11) apply (r. 65.10(1A)(b)).

DRINKING BANNING ORDERS

Parenting orders

93.24A   A magistrates' court or a county court may make a parenting order, under the Anti-social Behaviour Act 2003, s. 26A (on the application of a local authority) or s. 26B (on the application of a registered social landlord), in respect of a parent of a child or young person, if it is satisfied:

(a) that the child or young person has engaged in anti-social behaviour, and
(b) that making the order would be desirable in the interests of preventing the child or young person from engaging in further anti-social behaviour.

A parenting order is an order which requires the parent to comply, for a period not exceeding 12 months, with such requirements as are specified in the order (ss. 26A(3)(a) and 26B(3)(a)). If another parenting order has previously been made (under any enactment) in respect of the same parent, a requirement under s. 26A(3)(b) or s. 26B(3)(b) may be added that the parent must attend, for a concurrent period not exceeding three months, such counselling or guidance programme as may be specified in directions given by the responsible officer (defined in s. 26A(8) and s. 26B(9) and (10)). A counselling or guidance programme may be, or include, a residential course (ss. 26A(5) and 26B(5)), but only if the court is satisfied that the attendance of the parent at a residential course is likely to be more effective than attendance at a non-residential course in preventing the child or young person from engaging in further anti-social behaviour (ss. 26A(6) and 26B(6)). Also the court must be satisfied that any interference with family life which is likely to result from the attendance of the parent at a residential course is proportionate in all the circumstances (ss. 26A(7) and 26B(7)).

A registered social landlord must not make an application for a parenting order without first consulting the local authority in whose area the child or young person in question resides or appears to reside (s. 26B(8)).

Parenting orders incidental to county court proceedings

93.24B   The Anti-social Behaviour Act 2003, s. 26C, provides for parenting orders to be made in county court proceedings. The provisions are similar to those under which ASBOs may be made.

A 'relevant authority' may apply for a parenting order to be made, in county court proceedings to which it is a party (s. 26C(1)). A relevant authority may apply to be joined to proceedings for the purpose of making an application (s. 26C(2)). If it is a party to county court proceedings, it may apply for an individual to be joined in those proceedings so that it may apply for a parenting order, provided it considers that a child or young person of which that person is a parent has engaged in anti-social behaviour that is material to those proceedings (s. 26C(3)). No person under 18 may be joined (PD 65, para. 16.3).

For parenting orders the relevant authorities are local authorities and registered social landlords (Anti-social Behaviour Act 2003, s. 26C(1)).

Procedure

Any application for a parenting order to be made under the Anti-social Behaviour Act 2003, **93.24C** s. 26A or s. 26B, must be accompanied by written evidence (CPR, r. 65.41). If the application is by a registered social landlord, there must be evidence that it has consulted the relevant local authority in accordance with the Anti-social Behaviour Act 2003, s. 26B(8) (PD 65, para. 16.1). An application should be made as soon as possible after the relevant authority becomes aware of the circumstances which lead it to apply for a parenting order (CPR, rr. 65.38(2), 65.39(2)(a) and 65.40(1)(b)). The application must normally be on notice to the person against whom the parenting order is sought (rr. 65.38(3), 65.39(2)(b) and 65.40(4)).

If a relevant authority wishes to apply as a party to county court proceedings for a parenting order to be made against another party, it should make the application in its claim form or, if it is a defendant, in an application notice filed with the defence (r. 65.38(1)). If the relevant authority only becomes aware at a later stage of the need for a parenting order, it must apply for one as soon as possible by application notice (r. 65.38(2)).

An application to be joined to county court proceedings so as to apply for a parenting order to be made against one of the existing parties is an application for addition of a party and so must be made under Part 19, Section I (r. 65.39(1)(a)). It should be made in the same application notice as the application for the parenting order (r. 65.39(1)(b)).

An application to join a person to county court proceedings so that a parenting order may be made is an application for addition of a party and must be made under Part 19, Section I, but r. 19.2 does not apply (r. 65.40(2)). It should be made in the same application notice as the application for the parenting order (r. 65.40(1)(a)). It must contain the authority's reasons for claiming the anti-social behaviour of the child or young person is material in relation to the proceedings, and details of the behaviour alleged (r. 65.40(3)).

A parenting order may be made by a district judge (PD 2B, para. 8.1A).

Service

A parenting order made under the Anti-social Behaviour Act 2003, s. 26A or s. 26B, must be **93.24D** served personally on the defendant (PD 65, para. 16.2).

Supplement to Appendix 1
Civil Procedure Rules 1998 and Practice Directions

In the supplements to appendices 1 to 6 notes by the editors of *Blackstone's Civil Practice* are in italic type and the text of legislation is in upright type.

CPR Part 2   Application and Interpretation of the Rules

As from 1 October 2007, amendments are made by the Civil Procedure (Amendment) Rules 2007 (SI 2007/2204), r. 3. Entry 4 in the table following r. 2.1 is changed to:

4. Proceedings before the Court of Protection   Mental Capacity Act 2005, s. 51

In r. 2.3(1), patient *is changed to* protected party.

PD 2B   Practice Direction—Allocation of Cases to Levels of Judiciary

As from 1 October 2006, para. 8.1A is replaced by:

8.1A A district judge has jurisdiction to make an order under:
    (1) the Crime and Disorder Act 1998, s. 1B or 1D (anti-social behaviour);
    (2) the Anti-social Behaviour Act 2003, s. 26A, 26B or 26C (parenting orders); and
    (3) the Violent Crime Reduction Act 2006, s. 4 or 9 (drinking banning orders).

PD 4   Practice Direction—Forms

The following changes to PD 4 took effect on 1 October 2007. In para. 3.2, third sentence, form 100 (request for lodgment (general)) *is added to the list of Court Funds Office forms. A new form is added to table 1:*

N165   Certificate of notification/non-notification (appeals from the Court of Protection to the Court of Appeal) (PD 52, para. 21.12(6) to (8))

Form N242 is deleted, and the description of form N292 is changed to:

Order on settlement on behalf of child or protected party (PD 21, para. 10.3)

CPR Part 6   Service of Documents

As from 1 October 2007, amendments are made by the Civil Procedure (Amendment) Rules 2007 (SI 2007/2204), r. 4. In the first sentence of r. 6.6(1), and in r. 6.6(2), patient *is changed to* protected party. *The following table is substituted for the table in r. 6.6(1):*

Type of document	Nature of party	Persons to be served
Claim form	Child who is not also a protected party	One of the child's parents or guardians; or if there is no parent or guardian, an adult with whom the child resides or in whose care the child is.
Claim form	Protected party	One of the following persons with authority in relation to the protected party as: (i) the attorney under a registered enduring power of attorney, (ii) the donee of a lasting power of attorney, (iii) the deputy appointed by the Court of Protection; or if there is no such person, an adult with whom the protected party resides or in whose care the protected party is.
Application for an order appointing a litigation friend, where the child or protected party has no litigation friend	Child or protected party	See rule 21.8.
Any other document	Child or protected party	The litigation friend who is conducting the proceedings on behalf of the child or protected party.

PD 7   Practice Direction—How to Start Proceedings—The Claim Form

As from 1 October 2007, para. 3.5A is reworded as:

3.5A Where a claim which is to be served out of jurisdiction is one which the court has power to deal with under the Judgments Regulation (which has the same meaning as in r. 6.18(j)), the claim form and, when they are contained in a separate document, the particulars of claim must be endorsed with a statement that the court has power under that Regulation to deal with the claim and that no proceedings based on the same claim are pending between the parties in Scotland, Northern Ireland or another Regulation State (which has the same meaning as in r. 6.18(k)).

PD 7C   Practice Direction—Production Centre

As from 1 October 2007, in para. 2.3(6), patient *is changed to* protected party.

PD 7E   Practice Direction—Money Claim Online

As from 1 October 2007, in para.4(3)(a) and (5)(b), patient *is changed to* protected party. *The following note is added at the end of para. 4:*

('Protected party' has the same meaning as in r. 21.1(2).)

PD 8   Practice Direction—Alternative Procedure for Claims

As from 1 October 2007, in paras 3.1(1) and 6.1(1), patient *is changed to* protected party. *The table after para. 9.3 is deleted and a new para. 9.4 and table are inserted:*

9.4   For applications that may or must be brought in the High Court, where no other rule or practice direction assigns the application to a Division of the court, the table specifies the Division to which the application is assigned.

Type of claim or application	Paragraph of Section C	Division	Schedule rule
Application under the Bills of Sale Act 1878, s. 14 (rectification of register)	10A	Queen's Bench Central Office	
Application under the Bills of Sale Act 1878, s. 15 (entry of satisfaction)	11	Queen's Bench Central Office	
Application under the Bills of Sale Act 1878, s. 16 (search of the bills of sale register)	11A	Queen's Bench Central Office	
Application under the proviso to the Bills of Sale Act (1878) Amendment Act 1882, s. 7 (restraining removal or sale of goods seized)		Queen's Bench Central Office	
Application under the Public Trustee Act 1906 (free-standing proceedings)	12	Chancery	
Application under the Deeds of Arrangement Act 1914, s. 7 (rectification of register)	12A	Queen's Bench Central Office	
Applications under the Public Order Act 1936, s. 2(3)	13	Chancery	
Proceedings under jurisdiction conferred by the Railway and Canal Commission (Abolition) Act 1949, s. 1	14	Chancery	
Administration of Justice Act 1960 (applications under the Act)		Divisional Court	RSC, ord. 109, r. 1(3)
Administration of Justice Act 1960 (appeals under s. 13 of the Act)		Divisional Court	RSC, ord. 109, r. 2(4)
Proceedings under the Commons Registration Act 1965, s. 14		Chancery	
Application under the Mines (Working Facilities and Support) Act 1966	15	Chancery	
Proceedings under the Law of Property Act 1969, s. 21 or 25		Chancery	
Local Government Act 1972 (claims under s. 92—proceedings for disqualification)		Queen's Bench Central Office	

Type of claim or application	Paragraph of Section C	Division	Schedule rule
Application under the Mortgaging of Aircraft Order 1972 (SI 1972/1268), art. 10 (rectification of register)	15A	Chancery	
Application to register an assignment of book debts (Insolvency Act 1986, s. 344)	15B	Queen's Bench Central Office	
Proceedings under the Control of Misleading Advertisements Regulations 1988 (SI 1988/915)		Chancery	
Application under the Supreme Court Act 1981, s. 42	16	Administrative Court	
Proceedings in the High Court under the Representation of the People Acts	17A	Queen's Bench Central Office	
Applications under the Mental Health Act 1983, part II	18	Administrative Court	
Applications under the Coroners Act 1988, s. 13	19	Administrative Court	
Application for an injunction to prevent environmental harm under the Town and Country Planning Act 1990, s. 187B or 214A; the Planning (Listed Buildings and Conservation Areas) Act 1990, s. 44A; or the Planning (Hazardous Substances) Act 1990, s. 26AA	20	Queen's Bench	
Confiscation and forfeiture in connection with criminal proceedings (Drug Trafficking Act 1994 and Criminal Justice (International Co-operation) Act 1990—application for a confiscation order)		Queen's Bench	RSC, ord. 115, r. 2B(1)
Confiscation and forfeiture in connection with criminal proceedings (Drug Trafficking Act 1994 and Criminal Justice (International Co-operation) Act 1990—application for a restraint order or charging order)		Queen's Bench	RSC, ord. 115, r. 3(1)
Confiscation and forfeiture in connection with criminal proceedings (Drug Trafficking Act 1994 and Criminal Justice (International Co-operation) Act 1990—realisation of property)		Queen's Bench	RSC, ord. 115, r. 7(1)
Criminal Procedure and Investigations Act 1996 (application under s. 54(3))		Queen's Bench	RSC, ord. 116, r. 5(1)
Confiscation and forfeiture in connection with criminal proceedings (Terrorism Act 2000—application for a restraint order)		Queen's Bench	RSC, ord. 115, r. 26(1)
Proceedings under the Financial Services and Markets Act 2000	21	Chancery	
Interpleader (mode of application)		Chancery or Queen's Bench	RSC, ord. 17, r. 3(1)
Criminal proceedings (estreat of recognisances)		Queen's Bench	RSC, ord. 79, r. 8(2)
Criminal proceedings (bail)		Queen's Bench	RSC, ord. 79, r. 9(2)

Type of claim or application	Paragraph of Section C	Division	Schedule rule
Application under an enactment giving the High Court jurisdiction to quash or prohibit any order, scheme, certificate or plan, any amendment or approval of a plan, any decision of a Minister or government department or any action on the part of a Minister or government department	22	Administrative Court	

New paras 10A.1 to 10A.5 are inserted after para. 10.1:

Applications under Section 14 of the Bills of Sale Act 1878

10A.1 This paragraph applies to an application under the Bills of Sale Act 1878, s. 14, for an order to rectify an omission or misstatement in relation to the registration, or renewal of the registration, of a bill of sale:
  (1) by inserting in the register the true name, residence or occupation of a person; or
  (2) by extending the time for registration of the bill of sale or an affidavit of its renewal.
10A.2 The application must be made:
  (1) by claim form under Part 8; or
  (2) by witness statement.
10A.3 Where the application is made by witness statement:
  (1) Part 23 applies to the application;
  (2) the witness statement constitutes the application notice under that Part;
  (3) the witness statement does not need to be served on any other person; and
  (4) the application will normally be dealt with without a hearing.
10A.4 The application must set out:
  (1) the particulars of the bill of sale and of the omission or misstatement; and
  (2) the grounds on which the application is made.
10A.5 The application must be made to a master of the Queen's Bench Division and accompanied by payment of the prescribed fee.

New paras 11A.1 to 11A.4 are inserted after para. 11.5:

Applications under Section 16 of the Bills of Sale Act 1878

11A.1 This paragraph applies to an application under the Bills of Sale Act 1878, s. 16, for a search of the bills of sale register and for a certificate of the results of the search.
11A.2 The application must be made:
  (1) by claim form under Part 8; or
  (2) by written request.
11A.3 The application must give sufficient information to enable the relevant bill of sale to be identified.
11A.4 The application must be made to a master of the Queen's Bench Division and accompanied by payment of the prescribed fee.

New paras 12A.1 to 12A.5 are inserted after para. 12.2:

Applications under Section 7 of the Deeds of Arrangement Act 1914

12A.1 This paragraph applies to an application under the Deeds of Arrangement Act 1914, s. 7, for an order to rectify an omission or misstatement in relation to the registration of a deed of arrangement:
  (1) by inserting in the register the true name, residence or description of a person; or
  (2) by extending the time for registration.
12A.2 The application must be made:
  (1) by claim form under Part 8; or
  (2) by witness statement.

12A.3 Where the application is made by witness statement:
   (1) Part 23 applies to the application;
   (2) the witness statement constitutes the application notice under that Part;
   (3) the witness statement does not need to be served on any other person; and
   (4) the application will normally be dealt with without a hearing.
12A.4 The application must set out:
   (1) the particulars of the deed of arrangement and of the omission or misstatement; and
   (2) the grounds on which the application is made.
12A.5 The application must be made to a master of the Queen's Bench Division and accompanied by payment of the prescribed fee.

New paras 15A.1 to 15B.6 are inserted after para. 15.14:

Applications under Article 10 of the Mortgaging of Aircraft Order 1972

15A.1 This paragraph applies to an application under the Mortgaging of Aircraft Order 1972 (SI 1972/1268), art. 10, for an order to amend the Register of Aircraft Mortgages.
15A.2 The application must be made by claim form under Part 8.
15A.3 Every person (other than the claimant) who appears in the register as mortgagor or mortgagee of the aircraft concerned must be made a defendant to the claim.
15A.4 A copy of the claim form must be sent to the Civil Aviation Authority.
15A.5 The application will be assigned to the Chancery Division.
15A.6 The Civil Aviation Authority is entitled to be heard in the proceedings.

Applications under Section 344 of the Insolvency Act 1986 for Registration of Assignments of Book Debts

15B.1 This paragraph applies to an application under the Insolvency Act 1986, s. 344, to register an assignment of book debts.
15B.2 The application must be made:
   (1) by claim form under Part 8; or
   (2) by witness statement.
15B.3 The application must be made to a master of the Queen's Bench Division and accompanied by payment of the prescribed fee.
15B.4 Where the application is made by witness statement:
   (1) Part 23 applies to the application;
   (2) the witness statement constitutes the application notice under that Part;
   (3) the witness statement does not need to be served on any other person; and
   (4) the application will normally be dealt with without a hearing.
15B.5 The application:
   (1) must have exhibited to it a true copy of the assignment and of every schedule to it;
   (2) must set out the particulars of the assignment and the parties to it; and
   (3) must verify the date and time of the execution of the assignment, and its execution in the presence of a witness.
15B.6 Upon the court being satisfied, the documents so exhibited will be filed and the particulars of the assignment and of the parties to it entered in the register.

A new para. 17A.1 is inserted after para. 17.8:

Other Proceedings under the Representation of the People Acts

17A.1 (1) This paragraph applies to proceedings under the Representation of the People Acts (other than proceedings under the Representation of the People Act 1983, s. 30).
   (2) The jurisdiction of the High Court under those Acts in matters relating to Parliamentary and local government elections will be exercised by the Divisional Court except that:
      (a) any jurisdiction, under a provision of any of those Acts, exercisable by a single judge will be exercised by a single judge;
      (b) any jurisdiction, under any such provision, exercisable by a master will be exercised by a master; and

(c) where the court's jurisdiction in matters relating to Parliamentary elections is exercisable by a single judge, that jurisdiction in matters relating to local government elections is also exercisable by a single judge.

PD 10   Practice Direction—Acknowledgment of Service

As from 1 October 2007, in para.4.5, patients *is changed to* protected parties.

CPR Part 12   Default Judgment

As from 1 October 2007, amendments are made by the Civil Procedure (Amendment) Rules 2007 (SI 2007/2204), r. 5. In r. 12.10(a)(i) and r. 12.11(3), patient *is changed to* protected party.

PD 12   Practice Direction—Default Judgment

As from 1 October 2007, in para. 2.3(1), patients *is changed to* protected parties, *and in para. 4.2,* patient *is changed to* protected party *(in both places).*

CPR Part 14   Admissions

As from 1 October 2007, amendments are made by the Civil Procedure (Amendment) Rules 2007 (SI 2007/2204), r. 6. In r. 14.1(4), and in the cross-reference following r. 14.1(4), patient *is changed to* protected party.

CPR Part 19   Parties and Group Litigation

As from 1 October 2007, amendments are made by the Civil Procedure (Amendment) Rules 2007 (SI 2007/2204), r. 7 and sch. 1. Rule 19.9 is replaced by:

19.9 Derivative Claims—How Started

(1) This rule—
   (a) applies to a derivative claim (where a company, other body corporate or trade union is alleged to be entitled to claim a remedy, and a claim is made by a member of it for it to be given that remedy), whether under Chapter 1 of Part 11 of the Companies Act 2006 or otherwise; but
   (b) does not apply to a claim made pursuant to an order under [section 994*] of that Act.
(2) A derivative claim must be started by a claim form.

---

* The Queen's Printer's copy mistakenly refers to section 944.

(3) The company, body corporate or trade union for the benefit of which a remedy is sought must be made a defendant to the claim.

(4) After the issue of the claim form, the claimant must not take any further step in the proceedings without the permission of the court, other than—

(a) a step permitted or required by rule 19.9A or 19.9C; or

(b) making an urgent application for interim relief.

Rule 19.9 applies only to a derivative claim issued on or after 1 October 2007 (SI 2007/2204, r. 21(1)(a)).

19.9A Derivative Claims under Chapter 1 of Part 11 of the Companies Act 2006— Application for Permission

(1) In this rule—

'the Act' means the Companies Act 2006;

'derivative claim' means a derivative claim under Chapter 1 of Part 11 of the Act;

'permission application' means an application referred to in section 261(2), 262(2) or 264(2) of the Act;

'the company' means the company for the benefit of which the derivative claim is brought.

(2) When the claim form for a derivative claim is issued, the claimant must file—

(a) an application notice under Part 23 for permission to continue the claim; and

(b) the written evidence on which the claimant relies in support of the permission application.

(3) The claimant must not make the company a respondent to the permission application.

(4) Subject to paragraph (7), the claimant must notify the company of the claim and permission application by sending to the company as soon as reasonably practicable after the claim form is issued—

(a) a notice in the form set out in the practice direction supplementing this rule, and to which is attached a copy of the provisions of the Act required by that form;

(b) copies of the claim form and the particulars of claim;

(c) the application notice; and

(d) a copy of the evidence filed by the claimant in support of the permission application.

(5) The claimant may send the notice and documents required by paragraph (4) to the company by any method permitted by Part 6 as if the notice and documents were being served on the company.

(6) The claimant must file a witness statement confirming that the claimant has notified the company in accordance with paragraph (4).

(7) Where notifying the company of the permission application would be likely to frustrate some party† of the remedy sought, the court may, on application by the claimant, order that the company need not be notified for such period after the issue of the claim form as the court directs.

(8) An application under paragraph (7) may be made without notice.

(9) Where the court dismisses the claimant's permission application without a hearing, the court will notify the claimant and (unless the court orders otherwise) the company of that decision.

(10) The claimant may ask for an oral hearing to reconsider the decision to dismiss the permission application, but the claimant—

(a) must make the request to the court in writing within seven days of being notified of the decision; and

(b) must notify the company in writing, as soon as reasonably practicable, of that request unless the court orders otherwise.

(11) Where the court dismisses the permission application at a hearing pursuant to paragraph (10), it will notify the claimant and the company of its decision.

(12) Where the court does not dismiss the application under section 261(2) of the Act, the court will—

(a) order that the company and any other appropriate party must be made respondents to the permission application; and

(b) give directions for the service on the company and any other appropriate party of the application notice and the claim form.

---

† Perhaps 'party' should be 'part'.

Rule 19.9A applies only to a derivative claim issued on or after 1 October 2007 (SI 2007/2204, r. 21(1)(a)).

19.9B Derivative Claims under Chapter 1 of Part 11 of the Companies Act 2006— Members of Companies Taking over Claims by Companies or Other Members

(1) This rule applies to proceedings under section 262(1) or 264(1) of the Companies Act 2006.

(2) The application for permission must be made by an application notice in accordance with Part 23.

(3) Rule 19.9A (except for paragraphs (1), (2) and (4)(b) of that rule, and paragraph (12)(b) so far as it applies to the claim form) applies to an application under this rule and references to the claimant in rule 19.9A are to be read as references to the person who seeks to take over the claim.

Rule 19.9B applies to the taking over of a derivative claim only where the relevant application for permission to take over the claim is filed on or after 1 October 2007 (SI 2007/2204, r. 21(1)(b)).

19.9C Derivative Claims—Other Bodies Corporate and Trade Unions

(1) This rule sets out the procedure where—
  (a) either—
    (i) a body corporate to which Chapter 1 of Part 11 of the Companies Act 2006 does not apply; or
    (ii) a trade union,
  is alleged to be entitled to a remedy; and
  (b) either—
    (i) a claim is made by a member for it to be given that remedy; or
    (ii) a member of the body corporate or trade union seeks to take over a claim already started, by the body corporate or trade union or one or more of its members, for it to be given that remedy.

(2) The member who starts, or seeks to take over, the claim must apply to the court for permission to continue the claim.

(3) The application for permission must be made by an application notice in accordance with Part 23.

(4) The procedure for applications in relation to companies under section 261, 262 or 264 (as the case requires) of the Companies Act 2006 applies to the permission application as if the body corporate or trade union were a company.

(5) Rule 19.9A (except for paragraphs (1), (2) and (4)(b) of that rule, and paragraph (12)(b) so far as it applies to the claim form) also applies to the permission application as if the body corporate or trade union were a company.

Rule 19.9C applies to a derivative claim issued on or after 1 October 2007, and applies to the taking over of a derivative claim only where the relevant application for permission to take over the claim is filed on or after 1 October 2007 (SI 2007/2204, r. 21(1)(c)).

19.9D Derivative Claims Arising in the Course of Other Proceedings

If a derivative claim (except such a claim in pursuance of an order under section 994 of the Companies Act 2006) arises in the course of other proceedings—
(a) in the case of a derivative claim under Chapter 1 of Part 11 of that Act, rule 19.9A or 19.9B applies, as the case requires; and
(b) in any other case, rule 19.9C applies.

Rule 19.9D applies to a derivative claim that arises in the course of other proceedings only if:

(a) r. 19.9A would apply to the claim if it were brought; or

(b) r. 19.9B or 19.9C would apply to the taking over of the claim (SI 2007/2204, r. 21(1)(d)).

19.9E Derivative Claims—Costs

The court may order the company, body corporate or trade union for the benefit of which a derivative claim is brought to indemnify the claimant against liability for costs incurred in the permission application or in the derivative claim or both.

Rule 19.9E applies to a derivative claim only if r. 19.9A, 19.9B or 19.9C also applies to the claim (SI 2007/2204, r. 21(1)(e)).

19.9F Derivative Claims—Discontinuance and Settlement

Where the court has given permission to continue a derivative claim, the court may order that the claim may not be discontinued or settled without the permission of the court.

Rule 19.9F applies to a derivative claim only if r. 19.9A, 19.9B or 19.9C also applies to the claim (SI 2007/2204, r. 21(1)(e)).

Any derivative claim for which the claim form was issued before 1 October 2007 is subject to the rules of court relating to a derivative claim in force immediately before 1 October 2007 (SI 2007/2204, r. 21(2)).

PD 19C   Practice Direction—Derivative Claims

As from 1 October 2007, there is a new PD 19C:

PD 19C   Practice Direction—Derivative Claims

This practice direction supplements CPR, Part 19.

Application of This Practice Direction

1   This practice direction:
    (a) applies to:
        (i)   derivative claims, whether under the Companies Act 2006, part 11, ch. 1, or otherwise; and
        (ii) applications for permission to continue or take over such claims; but
    (b) does not apply to claims in pursuance of an order under s. 994 of that Act.

Claim Form

2   (1) A claim form must be headed 'Derivative claim'.
    (2) If the claimant seeks an order that the defendant company or other body concerned indemnify the claimant against liability for costs incurred in the permission application or the claim, this should be stated in the permission application or claim form or both, as the case requires.

Application for Order Delaying Notice

3   If the applicant seeks an order under r. 19.9A(7) delaying notice to the defendant company or other body concerned, the applicant must also:
    (a) state in the application notice the reasons for the application; and
    (b) file with it any written evidence in support of the application.

Form to Be Sent to Defendant Company or Other Body

4   The form required by r. 19.9A(4)(a) to be sent to the defendant company or other body is set out at the end of this practice direction. There are separate versions of the form for claims involving a company, and claims involving a body corporate of another kind or a trade union.

Early Intervention by the Company

5   The decision whether the claimant's evidence discloses a prima facie case will normally be made without submissions from or (in the case of an oral hearing to reconsider such a decision reached pursuant to r. 19.9A(9)) attendance by the company. If without invitation from the court the

company volunteers a submission or attendance, the company will not normally be allowed any costs of that submission or attendance.

(The Companies Act 2006, ss. 261, 262 and 264, contain provisions about disclosing a prima facie case in applications to continue a derivative claim.)

Hearing of Applications etc.

6   (1) Where a permission application to which this practice direction applies is made in the High Court it will be assigned to the Chancery Division and decided by a High Court judge.

(2) Where such an application is made in a county court it will be decided by a circuit judge.

Discontinuance of Derivative Claim

7   As a condition of granting permission to continue or take over a derivative claim, the court may order that the claim is not to be discontinued, settled or compromised without the court's permission. Such a condition may be appropriate where any future proposal to discontinue or settle might not come to the attention of members who might have an interest in taking over the claim.

Transitional Provisions

8   (1) From 1 October 2007 new rules came into force about procedures for derivative claims. The new rules are set out in CPR, rr. 19.9 to 19.9F.

(2) The rules of court in force immediately before 1 October 2007 apply to derivative claims begun before 1 October 2007. These (former r. 19.9) are set out below:

Derivative Claims

19.9 (1) This rule applies where a company, other incorporated body or trade union is alleged to be entitled to claim a remedy and a claim is made by one or more members of the company, body or trade union for it to be given that remedy (a 'derivative claim').

(2) The company, body or trade union for whose benefit a remedy is sought must be a defendant to the claim.

(3) After the claim form has been issued the claimant must apply to the court for permission to continue the claim and may not take any other step in the proceedings except—

(a) as provided by paragraph (5); or

(b) where the court gives permission.

(4) An application in accordance with paragraph (3) must be supported by written evidence.

(5) The—

(a) claim form;

(b) application notice; and

(c) written evidence in support of the application,

must be served on the defendant within the period within which the claim form must be served and, in any event, at least 14 days before the court is to deal with the application.

(6) If the court gives the claimant permission to continue the claim, the time within which the defence must be filed is 14 days after the date on which the permission is given or such period as the court may specify.

(7) The court may order the company, body or trade union to indemnify the claimant against any liability in respect of costs incurred in the claim.

THE FORMS

For Claims Involving a Company

Companies Act 2006, section 261 *or* 262 *or* 264

Civil Procedure Rules 1998, rule 19.9A(4)(c)

Notice in relation to derivative claim

To [*name of company etc.*] ('the company') in relation to a claim by
[*claimant*]

Attached to this notice are:
- a copy of the claim form to which this notice relates;
- an application under rule 19.9A of the Civil Procedure Rules 1998 for permission to continue the claim; and
- copies of the evidence to be relied on by the claimant in obtaining permission to continue the claim.

The claim is a derivative claim. The claimant must obtain the permission of the court under section 261 of the Companies Act 2006 to continue the claim. A brief summary of the procedure follows.

The court will make its initial decision on the basis of the evidence filed by the claimant (copies are attached to this notice) and at present the company does not need to acknowledge service, file a defence or become involved in any other way. Initially the court may make its decision on the documents only, without a hearing; if it dismisses the application, the claimant may request reconsideration of that decision at a hearing but even at that hearing no additional evidence will be taken into account. If the court considers that the evidence filed by the claimant does not disclose a prima facie case, it must dismiss the application. It may then make consequential orders. If it does not dismiss the application at that stage, the court will adjourn the application to allow the company to obtain and file evidence and be heard on the application, and will make any necessary orders.

The court will notify the company of the outcome of each stage of the process.

The factors that the court must take into account are set out in section 263 of the Act. A copy of sections 263(1) to (4) of the Act is attached.

For Claims Involving a Body Corporate That Is not a Company, or a Trade Union

Civil Procedure Rules 1998, rule 19.9A(4)(c)

Notice in relation to derivative claim

To [*name of body corporate etc.*] ('the corporation') [*or as appropriate*] in relation to a claim by
[*claimant*]

Attached to this notice are:
- a copy of the claim form to which this notice relates;
- an application under rule 19.9A of the Civil Procedure Rules 1998 for permission to continue the claim; and
- copies of the evidence to be relied on by the claimant in obtaining permission to continue the claim.

The claim is a derivative claim. Under the Civil Procedure Rules 1998, the claimant must obtain the permission of the court to continue the claim. A brief summary of the procedure follows.

The court will make its initial decision on the basis of the evidence filed by the claimant (copies are attached to this notice) and at present the [*corporation*] does not need to acknowledge service, file a defence or become involved in any other way. Initially the court may make its decision on the documents only, without a hearing; if it dismisses the application, the claimant may request reconsideration of that decision at a hearing but even at that hearing no additional evidence will be taken into account. If the court considers that the evidence filed by the claimant does not disclose a prima facie case, it will dismiss the application. It may then make consequential orders. If it does not dismiss the application at that stage, the court will adjourn the application to allow the corporation to obtain and file evidence and be heard on the application, and will make any necessary orders.

The court will notify the [*corporation*] of the outcome of each stage of the process.

CPR Part 21   Children and Protected Parties

As from 1 October 2007, a new Part 21 is substituted by the Civil Procedure (Amendment) Rules 2007 (SI 2007/2204), r. 8 and sch. 2:

CPR Part 21   Children and Protected Parties

21.1 Scope of this Part

(1) This Part—
    (a) contains special provisions which apply in proceedings involving children and protected parties;
    (b) sets out how a person becomes a litigation friend; and
    (c) does not apply to proceedings under Part 75 where one of the parties to the proceedings is a child.

(2) In this Part—
    (a) 'the 2005 Act' means the Mental Capacity Act 2005;
    (b) 'child' means a person under 18;
    (c) 'lacks capacity' means lacks capacity within the meaning of the 2005 Act;
    (d) 'protected party' means a party, or an intended party, who lacks capacity to conduct the proceedings;
    (e) 'protected beneficiary' means a protected party who lacks capacity to manage and control any money recovered by him or on his behalf or for his benefit in the proceedings.

(Rule 6.6 contains provisions about the service of documents on children and protected parties)

(Rule 48.5 deals with costs where money is payable by or to a child or protected party)

21.2 Requirement for a Litigation Friend in Proceedings by or against Children and Protected Parties

(1) A protected party must have a litigation friend to conduct proceedings on his behalf.
(2) A child must have a litigation friend to conduct proceedings on his behalf unless the court makes an order under paragraph (3).
(3) The court may make an order permitting a child to conduct proceedings without a litigation friend.
(4) An application for an order under paragraph (3)—
    (a) may be made by the child;
    (b) if the child already has a litigation friend, must be made on notice to the litigation friend; and
    (c) if the child has no litigation friend, may be made without notice.

(5) Where—
  (a) the court has made an order under paragraph (3); and
  (b) it subsequently appears to the court that it is desirable for a litigation friend to conduct the proceedings on behalf of the child,

the court may appoint a person to be the child's litigation friend.

21.3 Stage of Proceedings at Which a Litigation Friend Becomes Necessary

(1) This rule does not apply where the court has made an order under rule 21.2(3).
(2) A person may not, without the permission of the court—
  (a) make an application against a child or protected party before proceedings have started; or
  (b) take any step in proceedings except—
    (i) issuing and serving a claim form; or
    (ii) applying for the appointment of a litigation friend under rule 21.6,
  until the child or protected party has a litigation friend.
(3) If during proceedings a party lacks capacity to continue to conduct proceedings, no party may take any further step in the proceedings without the permission of the court until the protected party has a litigation friend.
(4) Any step taken before a child or protected party has a litigation friend has no effect unless the court orders otherwise.

21.4 Who May Be a Litigation Friend without a Court Order

(1) This rule does not apply if the court has appointed a person to be a litigation friend.
(2) A deputy appointed by the Court of Protection under the 2005 Act with power to conduct proceedings on the protected party's behalf is entitled to be the litigation friend of the protected party in any proceedings to which his power extends.
(3) If nobody has been appointed by the court or, in the case of a protected party, has been appointed as a deputy as set out in paragraph (2), a person may act as a litigation friend if he—
  (a) can fairly and competently conduct proceedings on behalf of the child or protected party;
  (b) has no interest adverse to that of the child or protected party; and
  (c) where the child or protected party is a claimant, undertakes to pay any costs which the child or protected party may be ordered to pay in relation to the proceedings, subject to any right he may have to be repaid from the assets of the child or protected party.

21.5 How a Person Becomes a Litigation Friend without a Court Order

(1) If the court has not appointed a litigation friend, a person who wishes to act as a litigation friend must follow the procedure set out in this rule.
(2) A deputy appointed by the Court of Protection under the 2005 Act with power to conduct proceedings on the protected party's behalf must file an official copy$^{(GL)}$ of the order of the Court of Protection which confers his power to act either—
  (a) where the deputy is to act as a litigation friend for a claimant, at the time the claim is made; or
  (b) where the deputy is to act as a litigation friend for a defendant, at the time when he first takes a step in the proceedings on behalf of the defendant.
(3) Any other person must file a certificate of suitability stating that he satisfies the conditions specified in rule 21.4(3) either—
  (a) where the person is to act as a litigation friend for a claimant, at the time when the claim is made; or
  (b) where the person is to act as a litigation friend for a defendant, at the time when he first takes a step in the proceedings on behalf of the defendant.
(4) The litigation friend must—
  (a) serve the certificate of suitability on every person on whom, in accordance with rule 6.6 (service on a parent, guardian etc.), the claim form should be served; and
  (b) file a certificate of service when he files the certificate of suitability.
(Rule 6.10 sets out the details to be contained in a certificate of service)

21.6 How a Person Becomes a Litigation Friend by Court Order

(1) The court may make an order appointing a litigation friend.

(2) An application for an order appointing a litigation friend may be made by—
    (a) a person who wishes to be the litigation friend; or
    (b) a party.

(3) Where—
    (a) a person makes a claim against a child or protected party;
    (b) the child or protected party has no litigation friend;
    (c) the court has not made an order under rule 21.2(3) (order that a child can conduct proceedings without a litigation friend); and
    (d) either—
        (i) someone who is not entitled to be a litigation friend files a defence; or
        (ii) the claimant wishes to take some step in the proceedings,
the claimant must apply to the court for an order appointing a litigation friend for the child or protected party.

(4) An application for an order appointing a litigation friend must be supported by evidence.

(5) The court may not appoint a litigation friend under this rule unless it is satisfied that the person to be appointed satisfies the conditions in rule 21.4(3).

21.7 Court's Power to Change a Litigation Friend and to Prevent a Person Acting as a Litigation Friend

(1) The court may—
    (a) direct that a person may not act as a litigation friend;
    (b) terminate a litigation friend's appointment; or
    (c) appoint a new litigation friend in substitution for an existing one.

(2) An application for an order under paragraph (1) must be supported by evidence.

(3) The court may not appoint a litigation friend under this rule unless it is satisfied that the person to be appointed satisfies the conditions in rule 21.4(3).

21.8 Appointment of a Litigation Friend by Court Order—Supplementary

(1) An application for an order under rule 21.6 or 21.7 must be served on every person on whom, in accordance with rule 6.6 (service on parent, guardian etc.), the claim form must be served.

(2) Where an application for an order under rule 21.6 is in respect of a protected party, the application must also be served on the protected party unless the court orders otherwise.

(3) An application for an order under rule 21.7 must also be served on—
    (a) the person who is the litigation friend, or who is purporting to act as the litigation friend, when the application is made; and
    (b) the person who it is proposed should be the litigation friend, if he is not the applicant.

(4) On an application for an order under rule 21.6 or 21.7, the court may appoint the person proposed or any other person who satisfies the conditions specified in rule 21.4(3).

21.9 Procedure where Appointment of a Litigation Friend Ceases

(1) When a child who is not a protected party reaches the age of 18, the litigation friend's appointment ceases.

(2) Where a protected party regains or acquires capacity to conduct the proceedings, the litigation friend's appointment continues until it is ended by court order.

(3) An application for an order under paragraph (2) may be made by—
    (a) the former protected party;
    (b) the litigation friend; or
    (c) a party.

(4) The child or protected party in respect of whom the appointment to act has ceased must serve notice on the other parties—
    (a) stating that the appointment of his litigation friend to act has ceased;
    (b) giving his address for service; and
    (c) stating whether or not he intends to carry on the proceedings.

(5) If the child or protected party does not serve the notice required by paragraph (4) within 28 days after the day on which the appointment of the litigation friend ceases the court may, on application, strike out[(GL)] any claim brought by or defence raised by the child or protected party.

(6) The liability of a litigation friend for costs continues until—

    (a) the person in respect of whom his appointment to act has ceased serves the notice referred to in paragraph (4); or

    (b) the litigation friend serves notice on the parties that his appointment to act has ceased.

21.10 Compromise etc. by or on Behalf of a Child or Protected Party

(1) Where a claim is made—

    (a) by or on behalf of a child or protected party; or

    (b) against a child or protected party,

no settlement, compromise or payment (including any voluntary interim payment) and no acceptance of money paid into court shall be valid, so far as it relates to the claim by, on behalf of or against the child or protected party, without the approval of the court.

(2) Where—

    (a) before proceedings in which a claim is made by or on behalf of, or against, a child or protected party (whether alone or with any other person) are begun, an agreement is reached for the settlement of the claim; and

    (b) the sole purpose of proceedings is to obtain the approval of the court to a settlement or compromise of the claim, the claim must—

        (i) be made using the procedure set out in Part 8 (alternative procedure for claims); and

        (ii) include a request to the court for approval of the settlement or compromise.

(3) In proceedings to which Section II of Part 45 applies, the court will not make an order for detailed assessment of the costs payable to the child or protected party but will assess the costs in the manner set out in that Section.

(Rule 48.5 contains provisions about costs where money is payable to a child or protected party)

21.11 Control of Money Recovered by or on Behalf of a Child or Protected Party

(1) Where in any proceedings—

    (a) money is recovered by or on behalf of or for the benefit of a child or protected party; or

    (b) money paid into court is accepted by or on behalf of a child or protected party, the money will be dealt with in accordance with directions given by the court under this rule and not otherwise.

(2) Directions given under this rule may provide that the money shall be wholly or partly paid into court and invested or otherwise dealt with.

(3) Where money is recovered by or on behalf of a protected party or money paid into court is accepted by or on behalf of a protected party, before giving directions in accordance with this rule, the court will first consider whether the protected party is a protected beneficiary.

21.12 Expenses Incurred by a Litigation Friend

(1) In proceedings to which rule 21.11 applies, a litigation friend who incurs expenses on behalf of a child or protected party in any proceedings is entitled on application to recover the amount paid or payable out of any money recovered or paid into court to the extent that it—

    (a) has been reasonably incurred; and

    (b) is reasonable in amount.

(2) Expenses may include all or part of—

    (a) an insurance premium, as defined by rule 43.2(1)(m); or

    (b) interest on a loan taken out to pay an insurance premium or other recoverable disbursement.

(3) No application may be made under the rule for expenses that—

    (a) are of a type that may be recoverable on an assessment of costs payable by or out of money belonging to a child or protected party; but

    (b) are disallowed in whole or in part on such an assessment.

(Expenses which are also 'costs' as defined in rule 43.2(1)(a) are dealt with under rule 48.5(2))

(4) In deciding whether the expenses were reasonably incurred and reasonable in amount, the court will have regard to all the circumstances of the case including the factors set out in rule 44.5(3).

(5) When the court is considering the factors to be taken into account in assessing the reasonableness of the expenses, it will have regard to the facts and circumstances as they reasonably appeared to the litigation friend or to the child's or protected party's legal representative when the expense was incurred.

(6) Where the claim is settled or compromised, or judgment is given, on terms that an amount not exceeding £5,000 is paid to the child or protected party, the total amount the litigation friend may recover under paragraph (1) must not exceed 25% of the sum so agreed or awarded, unless the court directs otherwise. Such total amount must not exceed 50% of the sum so agreed or awarded.

21.13 Appointment of a Guardian of a Child's Estate

(1) The court may appoint the Official Solicitor to be a guardian of a child's estate where—
    (a) money is paid into court on behalf of the child in accordance with directions given under rule 21.11 (control of money received by a child or protected party);
    (b) the Criminal Injuries Compensation Authority notifies the court that it has made or intends to make an award to the child;
    (c) a court or tribunal outside England and Wales notifies the court that it has ordered or intends to order that money be paid to the child;
    (d) the child is absolutely entitled to the proceeds of a pension fund; or
    (e) in any other case, such an appointment seems desirable to the court.

(2) The court may not appoint the Official Solicitor under this rule unless—
    (a) the persons with parental responsibility (within the meaning of section 3 of the Children Act 1989) agree; or
    (b) the court considers that their agreement can be dispensed with.

(3) The Official Solicitor's appointment may continue only until the child reaches 18.

PD 21   Practice Direction—Children and Protected Parties

As from 1 October 2007, PD 21 is replaced by a new practice direction:

PD 21   Practice Direction—Children and Protected Parties

This practice direction supplements CPR, Part 21.

General

1.1 In proceedings where one of the parties is a protected party, the protected party should be referred to in the title to the proceedings as 'A.B. (a protected party by C.D. his litigation friend)'.

1.2 In proceedings where one of the parties is a child, where:
    (1) the child has a litigation friend, the child should be referred to in the title to the proceedings as 'A.B. (a child by C.D. his litigation friend)'; or
    (2) the child is conducting the proceedings on his own behalf, the child should be referred to in the title as 'A.B. (a child)'.

1.3 A settlement of a claim by a child includes an agreement on a sum to be apportioned to a dependent child under the Fatal Accidents Act 1976.

The Litigation Friend

2.1 A person may become a litigation friend:
    (a) without a court order under r. 21.5, or
    (b) by a court order under r. 21.6.

2.2 A person who wishes to become a litigation friend without a court order pursuant to r. 21.5(3) must file a certificate of suitability in form N235:

(a) stating that he consents to act,

(b) stating that he knows or believes that the [claimant] [defendant] [is a child] [lacks capacity to conduct the proceedings],

(c) in the case of a protected party, stating the grounds of his belief and, if his belief is based upon medical opinion or the opinion of another suitably qualified expert, attaching any relevant document to the certificate,

(d) stating that he can fairly and competently conduct proceedings on behalf of the child or protected party and has no interest adverse to that of the child or protected party, and

(e) where the child or protected party is a claimant, undertaking to pay any costs which the child or protected party may be ordered to pay in relation to the proceedings, subject to any right he may have to be repaid from the assets of the child or protected party.

2.3 The certificate of suitability must be verified by a statement of truth.

(Part 22 contains provisions about statements of truth.)

2.4 The litigation friend is not required to serve the document referred to in para. 2.2(c) when he serves a certificate of suitability on the person to be served under r. 21.5(4)(a).

Application for a Court Order Appointing a Litigation Friend

3.1 Rule 21.6 sets out who may apply for an order appointing a litigation friend.

3.2 An application must be made in accordance with Part 23 and must be supported by evidence.

3.3 The evidence in support must satisfy the court that the proposed litigation friend—

(1) consents to act,

(2) can fairly and competently conduct proceedings on behalf of the child or protected party,

(3) has no interest adverse to that of the child or protected party, and

(4) where the child or protected party is a claimant, undertakes to pay any costs which the child or protected party may be ordered to pay in relation to the proceedings, subject to any right he may have to be repaid from the assets of the child or protected party.

3.4 Where it is sought to appoint the Official Solicitor as the litigation friend, provision must be made for payment of his charges.

Procedure Where the Need for a Litigation Friend Has Come to an End

4.1 Rule 21.9 deals with the situation where the need for a litigation friend comes to an end during the proceedings because either:

(1) a child who is not also a protected party reaches the age of 18 (full age) during the proceedings, or

(2) a protected party regains or acquires capacity to conduct the proceedings.

4.2 A child on reaching full age must serve on the other parties to the proceedings and file with the court a notice:

(1) stating that he has reached full age,

(2) stating that his litigation friend's appointment has ceased,

(3) giving an address for service, and

(4) stating whether or not he intends to carry on with or continue to defend the proceedings.

4.3 If the notice states that the child intends to carry on with or continue to defend the proceedings he must subsequently be described in the proceedings as 'A.B. (formerly a child but now of full age)'.

4.4 Whether or not a child having reached full age serves a notice in accordance with r. 21.9(4) and para. 4.2 above, a litigation friend may, at any time after the child has reached full age, serve a notice on the other parties that his appointment has ceased.

4.5 Where a protected party regains or acquires capacity to conduct the proceedings, an application under r. 21.9(3) must be made for an order under r. 21.9(2) that the litigation friend's appointment has ceased.

4.6 The application must be supported by the following evidence:

(1) a medical report or other suitably qualified expert's report indicating that the protected party has regained or acquired capacity to conduct the proceedings,

(2) a copy of any relevant order or declaration of the Court of Protection, and

(3) if the application is made by the protected party, a statement whether or not he intends to carry on with or continue to defend the proceedings.

4.7 An order under r. 21.9(2) must be served on the other parties to the proceedings. The former protected party must file with the court a notice:

(1) stating that his litigation friend's appointment has ceased,

(2) giving an address for service, and

(3) stating whether or not he intends to carry on with or continue to defend the proceedings.

Settlement or Compromise by or on Behalf of a Child or Protected Party before the Issue of Proceedings

5.1 Where a claim by or on behalf of a child or protected party has been dealt with by agreement before the issue of proceedings and only the approval of the court to the agreement is sought, the claim must, in addition to containing the details of the claim and satisfying the requirements of r. 21.10(2), include the following:

(1) subject to para. 5.3, the terms of the settlement or compromise or have attached to it a draft consent order in form N292;

(2) details of whether and to what extent the defendant admits liability;

(3) the age and occupation (if any) of the child or protected party;

(4) the litigation friend's approval of the proposed settlement or compromise;

(5) a copy of any financial advice relating to the proposed settlement; and

(6) in a personal injury case arising from an accident:

(a) details of the circumstances of the accident,

(b) any medical reports,

(c) where appropriate, a schedule of any past and future expenses and losses claimed and any other relevant information relating to the personal injury as set out in the practice direction which supplements Part 16 (statements of case), and

(d) where considerations of liability are raised:

(i) any evidence or reports in any criminal proceedings or in an inquest, and

(ii) details of any prosecution brought.

5.2 (1) An opinion on the merits of the settlement or compromise given by counsel or solicitor acting for the child or protected party must, except in very clear cases, be obtained.

(2) A copy of the opinion and, unless the instructions on which it was given are sufficiently set out in it, a copy of the instructions, must be supplied to the court.

5.3 Where in any personal injury case a claim for damages for future pecuniary loss is settled, the provisions in paras 5.4 and 5.5 must in addition be complied with.

5.4 The court must be satisfied that the parties have considered whether the damages should wholly or partly take the form of periodical payments.

5.5 Where the settlement includes provision for periodical payments, the claim must:

(1) set out the terms of the settlement or compromise; or

(2) have attached to it a draft consent order,

which must satisfy the requirements of rr. 41.8 and 41.9 as appropriate.

5.6 Applications for the approval of a settlement or compromise will normally be heard by:

(1) a master or a district judge in proceedings involving a child; and

(2) a master, designated civil judge or his nominee in proceedings involving a protected party.

(For information about provisional damages claims see Part 41 and PD 41.)

Settlement or Compromise by or on Behalf of a Child or Protected Party after Proceedings Have Been Issued

6.1 Where in any personal injury case a claim for damages for future pecuniary loss, by or on behalf of a child or protected party, is dealt with by agreement after proceedings have been issued, an application must be made for the court's approval of the agreement.

6.2 The court must be satisfied that the parties have considered whether the damages should wholly or partly take the form of periodical payments.

6.3 Where the settlement includes provision for periodical payments, an application under para. 6.1 must:

(1) set out the terms of the settlement or compromise; or

(2) have attached to it a draft consent order,

which must satisfy the requirements of rr. 41.8 and 41.9 as appropriate.

6.4 The court must be supplied with:

(1) an opinion on the merits of the settlement or compromise given by counsel or solicitor acting for the child or protected party, except in very clear cases; and

(2) a copy of any financial advice.

6.5 Applications for the approval of a settlement or compromise, except at the trial, will normally be heard by:

(1) a master or a district judge in proceedings involving a child; and

(2) a master, designated civil judge or his nominee in proceedings involving a protected party.

Apportionment under the Fatal Accidents Act 1976

7.1 A judgment on or settlement in respect of a claim under the Fatal Accidents Act 1976 must be apportioned between the persons by or on whose behalf the claim has been brought.

7.2 Where a claim is brought on behalf of a dependent child or children, any settlement (including an agreement on a sum to be apportioned to a dependent child under the Fatal Accidents Act 1976) must be approved by the court.

7.3 The money apportioned to any dependent child must be invested on the child's behalf in accordance with rr. 21.10 and 21.11 and paras 8 and 9 below.

7.4 In order to approve an apportionment of money to a dependent child, the court will require the following information:

(1) the matters set out in paras 5.1(2) and (3), and

(2) in respect of the deceased:

(a) where death was caused by an accident, the matters set out in paras 5.1(6)(a), (b) and (c), and

(b) his future loss of earnings, and

(3) the extent and nature of the dependency.

Control of Money Recovered by or on Behalf of a Child or Protected Party

8.1 When giving directions under r. 21.11, the court:

(1) may direct the money to be paid into court for investment,

(2) may direct that certain sums be paid direct to the child or protected beneficiary, his litigation friend or his legal representative for the immediate benefit of the child or protected beneficiary or for expenses incurred on his behalf, and

(3) may direct that the application in respect of the investment of the money be transferred to a local district registry.

8.2 The court will consider the general aims to be achieved for the money in court (the fund) by investment and will give directions as to the type of investment.

8.3 Where a child also lacks capacity to manage and control any money recovered by him or on his behalf in the proceedings, and is likely to remain so on reaching full age, his fund should be administered as a protected beneficiary's fund.

8.4 Where a child or protected beneficiary is in receipt of publicly funded legal services the fund will be subject to a first charge under the Access to Justice Act 1999, s. 10 (statutory charge), and an order for the investment of money on the child's or protected beneficiary's behalf must contain a direction to that effect.

Investment on Behalf of a Child

9.1 At the hearing of an application for the approval of a settlement or compromise the litigation friend or his legal representative must provide, in addition to the information required by paras 5 and 6:

(1) a CFO form 320 (initial application for investment of damages) for completion by the judge hearing the application; and

(2) any evidence or information which the litigation friend wishes the court to consider in relation to the investment of the award for damages.

9.2 Following the hearing in para. 9.1, the court will forward to the Court Funds Office a request for investment decision (form 212) and the Public Trustee's investment managers will make the appropriate investment.

9.3 Where an award for damages for a child is made at trial, unless para. 9.7 applies, the trial judge will:

(1) direct the money to be paid into court and placed into the special investment account until further investment directions have been given by the court;

(2) direct the litigation friend to make an application to a master or district judge for further investment directions; and

(3) give such other directions as the trial judge thinks fit, including a direction that the hearing of the application for further investment directions will be fixed for a date within 28 days from the date of the trial.

9.4 The application under para. 9.3(2) must be made by filing with the court:

(1) a completed CFO form 320; and

(2) any evidence or information which the litigation friend wishes the court to consider in relation to the investment of the award for damages.

9.5 The application must be sent in proceedings in the Royal Courts of Justice to the Masters' Support Unit (Room E16) at the Royal Courts of Justice.

9.6 If the application required by para. 9.3(2) is not made to the court, the money paid into court in accordance with para. 9.3(1) will remain in the special investment account subject to any further order of the court or para. 9.8.

9.7 If the money to be invested is very small the court may order it to be paid direct to the litigation friend to be put into a building society account (or similar) for the child's use.

9.8 If the money is invested in court, it must be paid out to the child on application when he reaches full age.

Investment on Behalf of a Protected Beneficiary

10.1 The Court of Protection has jurisdiction to make decisions in the best interests of a protected beneficiary. Fees may be charged for the administration of funds and these must be provided for in any settlement.

10.2 Where the sum to be administered for the benefit of the protected beneficiary is:

(1) £30,000 or more, unless a person with authority as:

(a) the attorney under a registered enduring power of attorney;

(b) the donee of a lasting power of attorney; or

(c) the deputy appointed by the Court of Protection,

to administer or manage the protected beneficiary's financial affairs has been appointed, the order approving the settlement will contain a direction to the litigation friend to apply to the Court of Protection for the appointment of a deputy, after which the fund will be dealt with as directed by the Court of Protection; or

(2) under £30,000, it may be retained in court and invested in the same way as the fund of a child.

10.3 A form of order transferring the fund to the Court of Protection is set out in form N292.

10.4 In order for the Court Funds Office to release a fund which is subject to the statutory charge, the litigation friend or his legal representative or the person with authority referred to in para. 10.2(1) must provide the appropriate regional office of the Legal Services Commission with an undertaking in respect of a sum to cover their costs, following which the regional office will advise the Court Funds Office in writing of that sum, enabling them to transfer the balance to the Court of Protection on receipt of a CFO form 200 payment schedule authorised by the court.

10.5 The CFO form 200 should be completed and presented to the court where the settlement or trial took place for authorisation, subject to paras 10.6 and 10.7.

10.6 Where the settlement took place in the Royal Courts of Justice the CFO form 200 must be completed and presented for authorisation:

(1) on behalf of a child, in the Masters' Support Unit, Room E105, and

(2) on behalf of a protected beneficiary, in the Judgment and Orders Section in the Action Department, Room E17.

10.7 Where the trial took place in the Royal Courts of Justice, the CFO form 200 is completed and authorised by the court officer.

Expenses Incurred by a Litigation Friend

11.1 A litigation friend may make a claim for expenses under r. 21.12(1):
  (1) where the court has ordered an assessment of costs under r. 48.5(2), at the detailed assessment hearing;
  (2) where the litigation friend's expenses are not of a type which would be recoverable as costs on an assessment of costs between the parties, to the master or district judge at the hearing to approve the settlement or compromise under Part 21 (the master or district judge may adjourn the matter to the costs judge); or
  (3) where an assessment of costs under r. 48.5(2) is not required, and no approval under Part 21 is necessary, by a Part 23 application supported by a witness statement to a costs judge or district judge as appropriate.
11.2 In all circumstances, the litigation friend must support a claim for expenses by filing a witness statement setting out:
  (1) the nature and amount of the expense; and
  (2) the reason the expense was incurred.

Guardian's Accounts

12. PD 40B, para. 8, deals with the approval of the accounts of a guardian of assets of a child.

Payment Out of Funds in Court

13.1 Applications to a master or district judge:
  (1) for payment out of money from the fund for the benefit of the child, or
  (2) to vary an investment strategy,
  may be dealt with without a hearing unless the court directs otherwise.
13.2 When the child reaches full age:
  (1) where his fund in court is a sum of money, it will be paid out to him on application; or
  (2) where his fund is in the form of investments other than money (for example shares or unit trusts), the investments will on application be:
    (a) sold and the proceeds of sale paid out to him; or
    (b) transferred into his name.
13.3 Where the fund is administered by the Court of Protection, any payment out of money from that fund must be in accordance with any decision or order of the Court of Protection.
13.4 If an application is required for the payment out of money from a fund administered by the Court of Protection, that application must be made to the Court of Protection.
(For further information on payments out of court, see PD 37.)

PD 22   Practice Direction—Statements of Truth

In footnote 2, patients *is changed to* protected parties.

PD 23   Practice Direction—Applications

As from 1 October 2007, in para. 6.2(c), less than one hour *is changed to* no more than one hour.

PD 23B   Practice Direction—Applications
under Particular Statutes

As from 1 October 2007, para. 1.1(3) is changed to:

(3) 'responsible adult' means—
   (a) in relation to a person under 16 to whom sub-paragraph (b) does not apply, the person having care and control of him;
   (b) in relation to a person who lacks capacity (within the meaning of the Mental Capacity Act 2005) to give his consent to tests—
      (i) a person having power under that Act to give consent on his behalf; or
      (ii) if there is no such person, the person with whom he resides or in whose care he is.

As from 1 October 2007, para. 1.2 is changed to:

1.2 Where an application is made for a direction in respect of a person who either—
   (a) is under 16; or
   (b) lacks capacity (within the meaning of the Mental Capacity Act 2005) to give his consent to the tests,
   the application notice must state the name and address of the responsible adult.

PD 25B   Practice Direction—Interim Payments

As from 1 October 2007, in para. 1.2, patient *is changed to* protected party, *and the following note is added after para. 1.2.*

('Child' and 'protected party' have the same meaning as in r. 21.1(2).)

PD 26B   Practice Direction—Pilot Scheme for Mediation
in Central London County Court

As from 1 October 2007, in para. 2(2)(a), patient *is changed to* protected party, *and the following note is added after para. 2(3).*

('Child' and 'protected party' have the same meaning as in r. 21.1(2).)

CPR Part 30   Transfer

As from 1 October 2007, an amendment is made by the Civil Procedure (Amendment) Rules 2007 (SI 2007/2204), r. 9. In r. 30.7, patient *is changed to* protected party.

CPR Part 32   Evidence

*As from 1 October 2007, an amendment is made by the Civil Procedure (Amendment) Rules 2007
(SI 2007/2204), r. 10. In r. 32.13(3)(e),* patient *is changed to* protected party.

CPR Part 36   Offers to Settle

*As from 1 October 2007, an amendment is made by the Civil Procedure (Amendment) Rules 2007
(SI 2007/2204), r. 11. The cross-reference after r. 36.9 is replaced by:*

(Rule 21.10 deals with compromise etc. by or on behalf of a child or protected party)

PD 37   Practice Direction—Miscellaneous Provisions about Payments into Court

As from 1 October 2007, para. 1.1 is replaced by:

1.1   Except where para. 1.2 applies, a party paying money into court under an order or in support of
a defence of tender before claim must:
(1) send to the Court Funds Office:
(a) the payment, usually a cheque made payable to the Accountant General of the
Supreme Court;
(b) a sealed copy of the order or a copy of the defence; and
(c) a completed Court Funds Office form 100;
(2) serve a copy of the form 100 on each other party; and
(3) file at the court:
(a) a copy of the form 100; and
(b) a certificate of service confirming service of a copy of that form on each party served.

The note after para. 2.2 is replaced by:

(Where money paid into court is accepted by or on behalf of a child or protected party, r. 21.11(1)(b)
provides that the money shall be dealt with in accordance with directions given by the court under
that rule and not otherwise. PD 21, paras 8 to 13, make further provision about how the money may
be dealt with.)

CPR Part 39   Miscellaneous Provisions Relating to Hearings

*As from 1 October 2007, an amendment is made by the Civil Procedure (Amendment) Rules 2007
(SI 2007/2204), r. 12. In r. 39.2(3)(d),* patient *is changed to* protected party.

PD 39   Practice Direction—Miscellaneous Provisions Relating to Hearings

As from 1 October 2007, in para. 1.6, patient *is replaced by* protected party *(on both occasions). A new para. 1.7A is inserted after para. 1.7:*

1.7A   Attention is drawn to PD 52, para. 24.5(8), which provides that an appeal to a county court against certain decisions under the Representation of the People Act 1983 is to be heard in private unless the court orders otherwise. Attention is also drawn to PD 52, para. 24.5(9), which provides that an appeal to the Court of Appeal against such a decision of a county court may be heard in private if the Court of Appeal so orders.

PD 40B   Practice Direction—Judgments and Orders

As from 1 October 2007, under the heading For Information About *at the end of the practice direction, in item (2),* patients *is replaced by* protected parties. *The erroneous reference has been corrected in the text issued by the Ministry of Justice.*

PD 41B   Practice Direction—Periodical Payments under the Damages Act 1996

As from 1 October 2007, in the heading to para. 7 and in para. 7 itself, patient *is changed to* protected party.

CPR Part 45   Fixed Costs

As from 1 October 2007, an amendment is made by the Civil Procedure (Amendment) Rules 2007 (SI 2007/2204), r. 13. In r. 45.10(2)(c), patient *is changed to* protected party.

CPR Part 46   Fast Track Trial Costs

As from 1 October 2007, amendments are made by the Civil Procedure (Amendment) Rules 2007 (SI 2007/2204), r. 14. In the cross-reference at the end of r. 46.1, patients *is changed to* protected parties. *The table in r. 46.2(1) is amended to:*

Value of the claim	Amount of fast track trial costs which the court may award
No more than £3,000	£485
More than £3,000 but not more than £10,000	£690
More than £10,000	£1,035

In r. 46.3(2)(c) £250 is increased to £345. In r. 46.3(4) £350 is increased to £485.

The amendments to rr. 46.2 and 46.3 apply only where the hearing of the fast track trial commences on or after 1 October 2007. Where the hearing commences before 1 October 2007, the rules of court relating to the amount of fast track trial costs which the court may award that were in force immediately before 1 October 2007 apply as if they had not been amended (SI 2007/2204, r. 22).

CPR Part 47   Procedure for Detailed Assessment of Costs and Default Provisions

As from 1 October 2007, amendments are made by the Civil Procedure (Amendment) Rules 2007 (SI 2007/2204), r. 15. In r. 47.3(1)(c), patient *is changed to* protected party*. In r. 47.22,* 14 days *is changed to* 21 days.

CPR Part 48   Costs—Special Cases

As from 1 October 2007, amendments are made by the Civil Procedure (Amendment) Rules 2007 (SI 2007/2204), r. 16. In r. 48.5, including its title, patient *is changed to* protected party *wherever it occurs. The cross-reference after r. 48.5(1) is replaced by:*

('Child' and 'protected party' have the same meaning as in rule 21.1(2))

PD 43–48   Practice Direction about Costs

As from 1 October 2007, in paras 1.5, 13.11(1) and (2), 21.15(2), 44.3(c) and 51.1, and in the heading to section 51, patient *is changed to* protected party.

CPR Part 49   Specialist Proceedings

As from 1 October 2007, an amendment is made by the Civil Procedure (Amendment) Rules 2007 (SI 2007/2204), r. 17. Rule 49(2) is replaced by:

(2) The proceedings referred to in paragraph (1) are proceedings under—
    (a) the Companies Act 1985;
    (b) the Companies Act 1989;
    (c) the Companies Act 2006; and
    (d) other legislation relating to companies.

PD 49B   Practice Direction—Applications under the Companies Act 1985 and Other Legislation Relating to Companies

As from 1 October 2007, PD 49B is replaced by new PD 49 and PD 49B:

PD 49   Practice Direction—Applications under the Companies Acts and Related Legislation

This practice direction supplements CPR, Part 49.

I GENERAL

Definitions

1   In this practice direction:
'the 1985 Act' means the Companies Act 1985;
'the 2006 Act' means the Companies Act 2006;
'the CJPA' means the Criminal Justice and Police Act 2001;
'the EC Regulation' means Council Regulation (EC) No. 2157/2001 of 8 October 2001 on the Statute for a European Company (SE);
'Part VII FSMA' means Part VII of the Financial Services and Markets Act 2000.

Application of This Practice Direction

2   This practice direction applies to proceedings under:
(a)   the 1985 Act;
(b)   the 2006 Act (except proceedings under part 11, ch. 1, or part 30);
(c)   the CJPA, s. 59;
(d)   the EC Regulation, arts 25 and 26; and
(e)   Part VII FSMA.
(CPR, Part 19, and PD 19C contain provisions about proceedings under the 2006 Act, part 11, ch. 1 (derivative claims).)

Application of This Practice Direction to Certain Proceedings in Relation to Limited Liability Partnerships

3   This practice direction applies to proceedings under the 1985 Act in relation to a limited liability partnership as if it were a company.

Title of Documents

4   (1)   The claim form in proceedings under the 1985 Act, the 2006 Act, Part VII FSMA or the EC Regulation, and any application, affidavit, witness statement, notice or other document in such proceedings, must be entitled:

In the matter of [*the name of the company in question*] and in the matter of [*the relevant law*]

where '[*the relevant law*]' means 'the Companies Act 1985', 'the Companies Act 2006', 'Part VII of the Financial Services and Markets Act 2000' or 'Council Regulation (EC) No. 2157/2001 of 8 October 2001 on the Statute for a European Company (SE)', as the case may be.
(2)   Where a company changes its name in the course of proceedings, the title must be altered by:
(a)   substituting the new name for the old; and
(b)   inserting the old name in brackets at the end of the title.

Starting Proceedings

5 (1) Proceedings to which this practice direction applies must be started by a Part 8 claim form:
  (a) unless a provision of this or another practice direction provides otherwise, but
  (b) subject to any modification of that procedure by this or any other practice direction.
 (2) The claim form:
  (a) will, where issued in the High Court, be issued out of the Companies Court or a Chancery district registry; or
  (b) will, where issued in a county court, be issued out of a county court office.

II PARTICULAR APPLICATIONS UNDER THE 1985 ACT

Applications under Section 721 of the 1985 Act (Production and Inspection of Books Where Offence Suspected)

6 (1) This paragraph applies to an application for an order under the 1985 Act, s. 721.
 (2) No notice need be given to, and the claim form need not be served on, any person against whom the order is sought.

Applications to Sanction Compromise or Arrangement

7 (1) This paragraph applies to an application for an order, under the 1985 Act, part XIII, to sanction a compromise or arrangement.
 (2) Where the application is made by the company concerned, or by a liquidator or administrator of the company, there need be no defendant to the claim unless the court so orders.
 (3) The claim form must be supported by written evidence including:
  (a) statutory information about the company; and
  (b) the terms of the proposed compromise or arrangement.
 (4) The claim form must seek:
  (a) directions for convening a meeting of creditors or members or both, as the case requires;
  (b) the sanction of the court to the compromise or arrangement, if it is approved at the meeting or meetings, and a direction for a further hearing for that purpose; and
  (c) a direction that the claimant files a copy of a report to the court by the chairman of the meeting or of each meeting.

III Particular Applications under the 2006 Act

References to Provisions of the 2006 Act in This Section

8 In this Section, a reference to a section by number, not otherwise identified, is to the section so numbered in the 2006 Act.

Company Generally to Be Made a Party to a Claim under the 2006 Act

9 (1) Where in a claim under the 2006 Act the company concerned is not the claimant, the company is to be made a defendant to the claim unless:
  (a) any other enactment, the CPR or this or another practice direction makes a different provision; or
  (b) the court orders otherwise.
 (2) Where an application is made in the course of proceedings to which the company is or is required to be a defendant, the company must be made a respondent to the application unless:
  (a) any other enactment, the CPR or this or another practice direction makes a different provision; or
  (b) the court orders otherwise.

Applications under Section 169 (Director's Right to Protest against Removal)

10 (1) This paragraph applies to an application for an order under s. 169(5).
 (2) The claimant:

(a) must serve a copy of the claim form on the company (if it is not the claimant) and on the director concerned; or

(b) if service is not reasonably practicable in the circumstances, must provide evidence that it has otherwise notified the company and that director of the application.

Applications under Section 295 (Application not to Circulate Members' Statement) or Section 317 (Application not to Circulate Members' Statement)

11 (1) This paragraph applies to an application for an order under s. 295 or 317.

(2) The claimant:

(a) must serve a copy of the claim form on the company (if it is not the claimant) and on each member who requested the circulation of the relevant statement; or

(b) if service is not reasonably practicable in the circumstances, must provide evidence that it has otherwise notified the company and each such member of the application.

Proceedings under Section 370 (Unauthorised Donations—Enforcement of Directors' Liabilities by Shareholder Action)

12 Proceedings to enforce a director's liability under s. 370 must be begun by a Part 7 claim form.

Proceedings under Section 955 (Takeovers—Enforcement by the Court)

13 Proceedings for an order under s. 955 must be begun by a Part 7 claim form.

Proceedings under Section 968 (Takeovers—Effect on Contractual Restrictions)

14. Proceedings to recover compensation under s. 968(6) must be begun by a Part 7 claim form.

Applications under Section 1132 (Production and Inspection of Documents Where Offence Suspected)

15 (1) This paragraph applies to an application for an order under s. 1132.

(2) No notice need be given to, and the claim form need not be served on, any person against whom the order is sought.

IV OTHER APPLICATIONS

Applications under the EC Regulation—Article 25

16 (1) In this paragraph and para. 17:

(a) a reference to an article by number is a reference to the article so numbered in the EC Regulation; and

(b) 'SE' means a European public limited-liability company (*Societas Europaea*) within the meaning of the EC Regulation.

(2) An application for a certificate under art. 25(2):

(a) must set out the pre-merger acts and formalities applicable to the applicant company;

(b) must be accompanied by evidence that those acts and formalities have been completed; and

(c) must be accompanied by copies of:

(i) the draft terms of merger, as provided for in art. 20;

(ii) the entry in the *Gazette* containing the particulars specified in art. 21;

(iii) a directors' report;

(iv) an expert's report; and

(v) the resolution of the applicant company approving the draft terms of merger in accordance with art. 23.

(3) In sub-para. (2)(c):

'directors' report' in relation to a company means a report by the directors of the company containing the information required by the 1985 Act, sch. 15B, para. 4;

'expert's report' in relation to a company means a report to the members of the company drawn up in accordance with:

(a) the 1985 Act, sch. 15B, para. 5; or

(b) art. 22.

(4) There need be no defendant to the claim.

Applications under the EC Regulation—Article 26

17 (1) Where under art. 26(2) a merging company is required to submit a certificate to the High Court, that company must, if no other merging company has begun proceedings under art. 26, begin such proceedings by issuing a claim form.

(2) There need be no defendant to the claim.

(3) The claim form:

(a) must name the SE and all of the merging companies;

(b) must be accompanied by the documents referred to in sub-para. (5); and

(c) must be served on each of the other merging companies.

(4) Where under art. 26(2) a merging company is required to submit a certificate to the High Court, and proceedings under art. 26 have already been begun, the company:

(a) must, not more than 14 days after service on it of the claim form, file an acknowledgment of service and serve it on each of the other merging companies; and

(b) must file the documents, in relation to each merging company, referred to in sub-para. (5) within the time limit specified in art. 26(2), and serve copies of them on each of the other merging companies.

(5) The documents in relation to each merging company are:

(a) the certificate issued under art. 25(2) in respect of the company;

(b) a copy of the draft terms of merger approved by the company;

(c) evidence that arrangements for employee involvement have been determined by the company pursuant to Council Directive 2001/86/EC of 8 October 2001 supplementing the Statute for a European company with regard to the involvement of employees; and

(d) evidence that the SE has been formed in accordance with art. 26(4).

Applications under Section 59 of the CJPA

18 (1) In sub-paras (2) to (8):

(a) a reference by number, not otherwise identified, is a reference to the provision so numbered in the CJPA; and

(b) references to a relevant interest in property have the same meaning as in the CJPA, s. 59.

(2) This paragraph applies to applications under s. 59 in respect of property seized in exercise of the power conferred by the 1985 Act, s. 448(3) (including any additional powers of seizure conferred by the CJPA, s. 50, that are exercisable by reference to that power).

(3) The application must be supported by evidence:

(a) that the claimant has a relevant interest in the property to which the application relates; and

(b) in the case of an application under s. 59(2), that one or more of the grounds set out in s. 59(3) is satisfied in relation to the property.

(4) Where the claimant has a relevant interest in the property, the defendants to the claim are to be:

(a) the person in possession of the property; and

(b) any other person who appears to have a relevant interest in the property.

(5) Where the claimant is in possession of the property, the defendants are to be:

(a) the person from whom the property was seized; and

(b) any other person who appears to have a relevant interest in the property.

(6) In the case of an application for the return of seized property, the claimant must serve a copy of the claim form and the claimant's evidence in support of it on the person specified, by the notice given under s. 52 when the property was seized, as the person to whom notice of such an application should be given.

(7) If the claimant knows the identity of the person who seized the property, the claimant must also notify that person of the application.

(8) When the court issues the claim form it will fix a date for the hearing.

V CONDUCT OF PROCEEDINGS

Reduction of Capital—Evidence

19   In the case of an application to confirm a reduction in capital, if any shares were issued otherwise than for cash:
   (a) for any shares so issued on or after 1 January 1901, it is sufficient to set out in the application the extent to which the shares are, or are treated as being, paid up; and
   (b) for any shares so issued between 1 September 1867 and 31 December 1900, the application must also show that the requirement as to the filing of the relevant contract with the Registrar of Joint Stock Companies in the Companies Act 1867, s. 25, was complied with.

VI MISCELLANEOUS

Service of Documents

20   The parties are responsible for service of documents in proceedings to which this practice direction applies.

Transitional Provisions

21   (1) A claim started, or an application made, before 1 October 2007 may be continued in accordance with the practice direction in force on 30 September 2007 as if it had not been revoked.
   (2) In particular, proceedings for the court to sanction a compromise or arrangement for which the relevant claim form was issued before 1 October 2007 may be continued in accordance with the practice direction in force on 30 September 2007 as if it had not been revoked.

PD 49B   Practice Direction—Order under Section 127 Insolvency Act 1986

This practice direction supplements CPR, Part 49.
1   Attention is drawn to the undesirability of asking as a matter of course for a winding-up order as an alternative to an order under [the Companies Act 2006, s. 994‡]. The petition should not ask for a winding-up order unless that is the remedy which the petitioner prefers or it is thought that it may be the only remedy to which the petitioner is entitled.
2   Whenever a winding-up order is asked for in a contributory's petition, the petition must state whether the petitioner consents or objects to an order under the Insolvency Act 1986, s. 127 ('a s.127 order'), in the standard form. If he objects, the written evidence in support must contain a short statement of his reasons.
3   If the petitioner objects to a s.127 order in the standard form but consents to such an order in a modified form, the petition must set out in the form of order to which he consents, and the written evidence in support must contain a short statement of his reasons for seeking the modification.
4   If the petition contains a statement that the petitioner consents to a s.127 order, whether in the standard or a modified form, but the petitioner changes his mind before the first hearing of the petition, he must notify the respondents and may apply on notice to a judge for an order directing that no s.127 order or a modified order only (as the case may be) shall be made by the registrar, but validating dispositions made without notice of the order made by the judge.
5   If the petition contains a statement that the petitioner consents to a s.127 order, whether in the standard or a modified form, the registrar shall without further enquiry make an order in such

---

‡ The text issued by the Ministry to Justice refers to the Companies Act 1985, s. 459.

form at the first hearing unless an order to the contrary has been made by the judge in the meantime.

6   If the petition contains a statement that the petitioner objects to a s.127 order in the standard form, the company may apply (in the case of urgency, without notice) to the judge for an order.

7   Section 127 Order – Standard Form:

Title etc.

ORDER that notwithstanding the presentation of the said Petition

(1)   payments made into or out of the bank accounts of the Company in the ordinary course of business of the Company and

(2)   dispositions of the property of the Company made in the ordinary course of its business for proper value between the date of presentation of the Petition and the date of judgment on the Petition or further order in the meantime shall not be void by virtue of the provisions of section 127 of the Insolvency Act 1986 in the event of an Order for the winding up of the Company being made on the said Petition provided that [*the relevant bank*] shall be under no obligation to verify for itself whether any transaction through the company's bank accounts is in the ordinary course of business, or that it represents full market value for the relevant transaction.

This form of Order may be departed from where the circumstances of the case require.

CPR Part 52   Appeals

As from 1 October 2007, amendments are made by the Civil Procedure (Amendment) Rules 2007 (SI 2007/2204), r. 18. A new r. 52.12A is inserted after r. 52.12:

52.12A Statutory Appeals—Court's Power to Hear Any Person

(1)   In a statutory appeal, any person may apply for permission—
(a)   to file evidence; or
(b)   to make representations at the appeal hearing.

(2)   An application under paragraph (1) must be made promptly.

New rr. 52.18, 52.19 and 52.20 are inserted after r. 52.17:

VI STATUTORY RIGHTS OF APPEAL

52.18 Appeals under the Law of Property Act 1922

An appeal lies to the High Court against a decision of the Secretary of State under paragraph 16 of Schedule 15 to the Law of Property Act 1922.

52.19 Appeals from Certain Tribunals

(1)   A person who was a party to proceedings before a tribunal referred to in section 11(1) of the Tribunals and Inquiries Act 1992 and is dissatisfied in point of law with the decision of the tribunal may appeal to the High Court.

(2)   The tribunal may, of its own initiative or at the request of a party to the proceedings before it, state, in the form of a special case for the decision of the High Court, a question of law arising in the course of the proceedings.

52.20 Appeals under Certain Planning Legislation

(1)   Where the Secretary of State has given a decision in proceedings on an appeal under Part VII of the Town and Country Planning Act 1990 against an enforcement notice—
(a)   the appellant;
(b)   the local planning authority; or
(c)   another person having an interest in the land to which the notice relates,
may appeal to the High Court against the decision on a point of law.

(2) Where the Secretary of State has given a decision in proceedings on an appeal under Part VIII of that Act against a notice under section 207 of that Act—
(a) the appellant;
(b) the local planning authority; or
(c) any person (other than the appellant) on whom the notice was served,
may appeal to the High Court against the decision on a point of law.
(3) Where the Secretary of State has given a decision in proceedings on an appeal under section 39 of the Planning (Listed Buildings and Conservation Areas) Act 1990 against a listed building enforcement notice—
(a) the appellant;
(b) the local planning authority; or
(c) any other person having an interest in the land to which the notice relates,
may appeal to the High Court against the decision on a point of law.

PD 52   Practice Direction—Appeals

As from 1 October 2007, PD 52 is amended as follows. Paragraphs 12.1 to 13.4 are replaced by:

12.1 These paragraphs do not apply where—
(1) any party to the proceedings is a child or protected party; or
(2) the appeal or application is to the Court of Appeal from a decision of the Court of Protection.
12.2 Where an appellant does not wish to pursue an application or an appeal, he may request the appeal court for an order that his application or appeal be dismissed. Such a request must contain a statement that the appellant is not a child or protected party and that the appeal or application is not from a decision of the Court of Protection. If such a request is granted it will usually be on the basis that the appellant pays the costs of the application or appeal.
12.3 If the appellant wishes to have the application or appeal dismissed without costs, his request must be accompanied by a consent signed by the respondent or his legal representative stating:
(1) that the respondent is not a child or protected party and that the appeal or application is not from a decision of the Court of Protection; and
(2) that he consents to the dismissal of the application or appeal without costs.
12.4 Where a settlement has been reached disposing of the application or appeal, the parties may make a joint request to the court stating that:
(1) none of them is a child or protected party; and
(2) the appeal or application is not from a decision of the Court of Protection,
and asking that the application or appeal be dismissed by consent. If the request is granted the application or appeal will be dismissed.
('Child' and 'protected party' have the same meaning as in r. 21.1(2).)
13.1 The appeal court will not normally make an order allowing an appeal unless satisfied that the decision of the lower court was wrong, but the appeal court may set aside or vary the order of the lower court with consent and without determining the merits of the appeal, if it is satisfied that there are good and sufficient reasons for doing so. Where the appeal court is requested by all parties to allow an application or an appeal the court may consider the request on the papers. The request should state that none of the parties is a child or protected party and that the application or appeal is not from a decision of the Court of Protection and set out the relevant history of the proceedings and the matters relied on as justifying the proposed order and be accompanied by a copy of the proposed order.

Procedure for consent orders and agreements to pay periodical payments involving a child or protected party or in applications or appeals to the Court of Appeal from a decision of the Court of Protection

13.2 Where one of the parties is a child or protected party or in applications or appeals to the Court
of Appeal from a decision of the Court of Protection:
(1) a settlement relating to an appeal or application;
(2) in a personal injury claim for damages for future pecuniary loss, an agreement reached at
the appeal stage to pay periodical payments; or
(3) a request by an appellant for an order that his application or appeal be dismissed with or
without the consent of the respondent,
requires the court's approval.

Child

13.3 In cases involving a child a copy of the proposed order signed by the parties' solicitors should be
sent to the appeal court, together with an opinion from the advocate acting on behalf of the
child.

Protected party

13.4 Where a party is a protected party the same procedure will be adopted, but the documents filed
should also include any relevant reports prepared for the Court of Protection.
('Child' and 'protected party' have the same meaning as in r. 21.1(2).)

In para. 16.1, the reference to paras 17.1–17.6 *is replaced by a reference to* paras 17.1–17.11.

Paragraph 17.5 is replaced by:

17.5 (1) In addition to the respondents to the appeal, the appellant must serve the appellant's
notice in accordance with r. 52.4(3) on the chairman of the tribunal, minister of State,
government department or other person from whose decision the appeal is brought.
(2) In the case of an appeal from the decision of a tribunal that has no chairman or member
who acts as a chairman, the appellant's notice must be served on the member or members
of the tribunal.

New rr. 17.7 to 17.11 are inserted after para. 17.6:

Rule 52.12A Statutory appeals—court's power to hear any person

17.7 Where all the parties consent, the court may deal with an application under r. 52.12A without
a hearing.

17.8 Where the court gives permission for a person to file evidence or to make representations at
the appeal hearing, it may do so on conditions and may give case management directions.

17.9 An application for permission must be made by letter to the relevant court office, identifying
the appeal, explaining who the applicant is and indicating why and in what form the applicant wants to participate in the hearing.

17.10 If the applicant is seeking a prospective order as to costs, the letter must say what kind of order
and on what grounds.

17.11 Applications to intervene must be made at the earliest reasonable opportunity, since it will
usually be essential not to delay the hearing.

Paragraph 18.8 is replaced by:

18.8 (1) A case stated by a tribunal must be signed by:
(a) the chairman;
(b) the president; or
(c) in the case where the tribunal has neither person in sub-para. (1)(a) or (b) nor any
member who acts as its chairman or president, by the member or members of the
tribunal.
(2) A case stated by any other person must be signed by that person or by a person authorised
to do so.

The following new entries are added to the table after para. 20.3:

Court of Protection	21.12
Proscribed Organisations Appeal Commission	21.11

Employment Tribunals Act 1996	22.6E
National Health Service Act 1977	22.6D
Planning (Listed Buildings and Conservation Areas) Act 1990, s. 65 (appeal)	22.6C
Planning (Listed Buildings and Conservation Areas) Act 1990, s. 65 (case stated)	22.8A
Town and Country Planning Act 1990, s. 289 (appeal)	22.6C
Town and Country Planning Act 1990, s. 289 (case stated)	22.8A
Representation of the People Act 1983, s. 56	24.4 to 24.6

New para. 21.12 is inserted after para. 21.11:

Appeal from the Court of Protection
21.12 (1) In this paragraph:
   (a) 'P' means a person who lacks, or who is alleged to lack, capacity within the meaning of the Mental Capacity Act 2005 to make a decision or decisions in relation to any matter that is subject to an order of the Court of Protection;
   (b) 'the person effecting notification' means:
      (i) the appellant;
      (ii) an agent duly appointed by the appellant; or
      (iii) such other person as the Court of Protection may direct,
      who is required to notify P in accordance with this paragraph; and
   (c) 'final order' means a decision of the Court of Appeal that finally determines the appeal proceedings before it.
(2) Where P is not a party to the proceedings, unless the Court of Appeal directs otherwise, the person effecting notification must notify P:
   (a) that an appellant's notice has been filed with the Court of Appeal and:
      (i) who the appellant is;
      (ii) what final order the appellant is seeking;
      (iii) what will happen if the Court of Appeal makes the final order sought by the appellant; and
      (iv) that P may apply under r. 52.12A by letter for permission to file evidence or make representations at the appeal hearing;
   (b) of the final order, the effect of the final order and what steps P can take in relation to it; and
   (c) of such other events and documents as the Court of Appeal may direct.
   (Paragraphs 17.7 to 17.11 of this practice direction contain provisions on how a third party can apply for permission to file evidence or make representations at an appeal hearing.)
(3) The person effecting notification must provide P with the information specified in sub-para. (2):
   (a) within 14 days of the date on which the appellant's notice was filed with the Court of Appeal;
   (b) within 14 days of the date on which the final order was made; or
   (c) within such time as the Court of Appeal may direct,
   as the case may be.
(4) The person effecting notification must provide P in person with the information specified in sub-para. (2) in a way that is appropriate to P's circumstances (for example, using simple language, visual aids or any other appropriate means).
(5) Where P is to be notified as to:
   (a) the existence or effect of a document other than the appellant's notice or final order; or
   (b) the taking place of an event,
      the person effecting notification must explain to P:
      (i) in the case of a document, what the document is and what effect, if any, it has; or
      (ii) in the case of an event, what the event is and its relevance to P.

(6) The person effecting notification must, within seven days of notifying P, file a certificate of notification (form N165) which certifies:
   (a) the date on which P was notified; and
   (b) that P was notified in accordance with this paragraph.
(7) Where the person effecting notification has not notified P in accordance with this paragraph, he must file with the Court of Appeal a certificate of non-notification (form N165) stating the reason why notification has not been effected.
(8) Where the person effecting notification must file a certificate of non-notification with the Court of Appeal, he must file the certificate within the following time limits:
   (a) where P is to be notified in accordance with sub-para. (2)(a) (appellant's notice), within 21 days of the appellant's notice being filed with the Court of Appeal;
   (b) where P is to be notified in accordance with sub-para. (2)(b) (final order), within 21 days of the final order being made by the Court of Appeal; or
   (c) where P is to be notified of such other events and documents as may be directed by the Court of Appeal, within such time as the Court of Appeal directs.
(9) The appellant or such other person as the Court of Appeal may direct may apply to the Court of Appeal seeking an order:
   (a) dispensing with the requirement to comply with the provisions of this paragraph; or
   (b) requiring some other person to comply with the provisions of this paragraph.
(10) An application made under sub-para. (9) may be made in the appellant's notice or by Part 23 application notice.
(Paragraph 12 contains provisions about the dismissal of applications or appeals by consent. Paragraph 13 contains provisions about allowing unopposed appeals or applications on paper and procedures for consent orders and agreements to pay periodical payments involving a child or protected party or in appeals to the Court of Appeal from a decision of the Court of Protection.)

New paras 22.6C to 22.6E are inserted after para. 22.6B:

Appeals under Section 289(6) of the Town and Country Planning Act 1990 and Section 65(5) of the Planning (Listed Buildings and Conservation Areas) Act 1990
22.6C (1) An application for permission to appeal to the High Court under the Town and Country Planning Act 1990 ('the TCP Act'), s. 289, or the Planning (Listed Buildings and Conservation Areas) Act 1990 ('the PLBCA Act'), s. 65, must be made within 28 days after notice of the decision is given to the applicant.
   (2) The application:
      (a) must be in writing and must set out the reasons why permission should be granted; and
      (b) if the time for applying has expired, must include an application to extend the time for applying, and must set out the reasons why the application was not made within that time.
   (3) The applicant must, before filing the application, serve a copy of it on the persons referred to in sub-para. (11) with the draft appellant's notice and a copy of the witness statement or affidavit to be filed with the application.
   (4) The applicant must file the application in the Administrative Court Office with:
      (i) a copy of the decision being appealed;
      (ii) a draft appellant's notice;
      (iii) a witness statement or affidavit verifying any facts relied on; and
      (iv) a witness statement or affidavit giving the name and address of, and the place and date of service on, each person who has been served with the application. If any person who ought to be served has not been served, the witness statement or affidavit must state that fact and the reason why the person was not served.
   (5) An application will be heard:
      (a) by a single judge; and
      (b) unless the court otherwise orders, not less than 21 days after it was filed at the Administrative Court Office.
   (6) Any person served with the application is entitled to appear and be heard.

(7) Any respondent who intends to use a witness statement or affidavit at the hearing:

  (a) must file it in the Administrative Court Office; and

  (b) must serve a copy on the applicant as soon as is practicable and in any event, unless the court otherwise allows, at least two days before the hearing.

(8) The court may allow the applicant to use a further witness statement or affidavit.

(9) Where on the hearing of an application the court is of the opinion that a person who ought to have been served has not been served, the court may adjourn the hearing, on such terms as it directs, in order that the application may be served on that person.

(10) Where the court grants permission:

  (a) it may impose terms as to costs and as to giving security;

  (b) it may give directions; and

  (c) the relevant appellant's notice must be served and filed within seven days of the grant.

(11) The persons to be served with the appellant's notice are:

  (a) the Secretary of State;

  (b) the local planning authority who served the notice or gave the decision, as the case may be, or, where the appeal is brought by that authority, the appellant or applicant in the proceedings in which the decision appealed against was given;

  (c) in the case of an appeal brought by virtue of the TCP Act, s. 289(1), or the PLBCA Act, s. 65(1), any other person having an interest in the land to which the notice relates; and

  (d) in the case of an appeal brought by virtue of the TCP Act, s. 289(2), any other person on whom the notice to which those proceedings related was served.

(12) The appeal will be heard and determined by a single judge unless the court directs that the matter be heard and determined by a Divisional Court.

(13) The court may remit the matter to the Secretary of State to the extent necessary to enable him to provide the court with such further information in connection with the matter as the court may direct.

(14) Where the court is of the opinion that the decision appealed against was erroneous in point of law, it will not set aside or vary that decision but will remit the matter to the Secretary of State for rehearing and determination in accordance with the opinion of the court.

(15) The court may give directions as to the exercise, until an appeal brought by virtue of the TCP Act, s. 289(1), is finally concluded and any rehearing and determination by the Secretary of State has taken place, of the power to serve, and institute proceedings (including criminal proceedings) concerning:

  (a) a stop notice under s. 183 of that Act; and

  (b) a breach of condition notice under s. 187A of that Act.

National Health Service Act 1977: appeal from tribunal

22.6D (1) This paragraph applies to an appeal from a tribunal constituted under the National Health Service Act 1977, s. 46.

  (2) The appellant must file the appellant's notice at the High Court within 14 days after the date of the decision of the tribunal.

Employment Tribunals Act 1996: appeal from tribunal

22.6E (1) This paragraph applies to an appeal from a tribunal constituted under the Employment Tribunals Act 1996, s. 1.

  (2) The appellant must file the appellant's notice at the High Court within 42 days after the date of the decision of the tribunal.

  (3) The appellant must serve the appellant's notice on the secretary of the tribunal.

A new para. 22.8A is inserted after para. 22.8:

Case stated under section 289 of the Town and Country Planning Act 1990 or section 65 of the Planning (Listed Buildings and Conservation Areas) Act 1990

22.8A A case stated under the Town and Country Planning Act 1990, s. 289(3), or the Planning (Listed Buildings and Conservation Areas) Act 1990, s. 65(2), will be heard and determined by a single judge unless the court directs that the matter be heard and determined by a Divisional Court.

Paragraph 23.9 is replaced by:

23.9 (1) A person aggrieved by the decision of a Commons Commissioner who requires the Commissioner to state a case for the opinion of the High Court under the Commons Registration Act 1965, s. 18, must file the appellant's notice within 42 days from the date on which notice of the decision was sent to the aggrieved person.

(2) Proceedings under that section are assigned to the Chancery Division.

New paras 24.4 to 24.6 are inserted after para. 24.3:

Representation of the People Act 1983—appeals against decisions of registration officers

24.4 (1) This paragraph applies in relation to an appeal against a decision of a registration officer, being a decision referred to in the Representation of the People Act 1983 ('the Act'), s. 56(1).

(2) Where a person ('the appellant') has given notice of such an appeal in accordance with the relevant requirements of s. 56, and of the regulations made under s. 53 ('the Regulations'), of the Act, the registration officer must, within seven days after he receives the notice, forward:

(a) the notice; and

(b) the statement required by the Regulations,

by post to the county court.

(3) The respondents to the appeal will be:

(a) the registration officer; and

(b) if the decision of the registration officer was given in favour of any other person than the appellant, that other person.

(4) On the hearing of the appeal:

(a) the statement forwarded to the court by the registration officer, and any document containing information submitted to the court by the registration officer pursuant to the Regulations, are admissible as evidence of the facts stated in them; and

(b) the court:

(i) may draw any inference of fact that the registration officer might have drawn; and

(ii) may give any decision and make any order that the registration officer ought to have given or made.

(5) A respondent to an appeal (other than the registration officer) is not liable for nor entitled to costs, unless he appears before the court in support of the registration officer's decision.

(6) Rule 52.4, and paras 5, 6 and 7 of this practice direction, do not apply to an appeal to which this paragraph applies.

Representation of the People Act 1983—special provision in relation to anonymous entries in the register

24.5 (1) In this paragraph:

'anonymous entry' has the meaning given by the Representation of the People Act 1983, s. 9B(4);

'appeal notice' means the notice required by the Representation of the People (England and Wales) Regulations 2001 (SI 2001/341), reg. 32.

(2) This paragraph applies to an appeal to a county court to which para. 24.4 applies if a party to the appeal is a person:

(a) whose entry in the register is an anonymous entry; or

(b) who has applied for such an entry.

(3) This paragraph also applies to an appeal to the Court of Appeal from a decision of a county court in an appeal to which para. 24.4 applies.

(4) The appellant may indicate in his appeal notice that he has applied for an anonymous entry, or that his entry in the register is an anonymous entry.

(5) The respondent or any other person who applies to become a party to the proceedings may indicate in a respondent's notice or an application to join the proceedings that his entry in the register is an anonymous entry, or that he has applied for an anonymous entry.

(6) Where the appellant gives such an indication in his appeal notice, the court will refer the matter to a district judge for directions about the further conduct of the proceedings, and, in particular, directions about how the matter should be listed in the court list.

(7) Where the court otherwise becomes aware that a party to the appeal is a person referred to in sub-para. (2), the court will give notice to the parties that no further step is to be taken until the court has given any necessary directions for the further conduct of the matter.

(8) In the case of proceedings in a county court, the hearing will be in private unless the court orders otherwise.

(9) In the case of proceedings in the Court of Appeal, the hearing may be in private if the court so orders.

Representation of the People Act 1983—appeals selected as test cases

24.6 (1) Where two or more appeals to which para. 24.4 applies involve the same point of law, the court may direct that one appeal ('the test-case appeal') is to be heard first as a test case.

(2) The court will send a notice of the direction to each party to all of those appeals.

(3) Where any party to an appeal other than the test-case appeal gives notice to the court, within seven days after the notice is served on him, that he desires the appeal to which he is a party to be heard:
  (a) the court will hear that appeal after the test-case appeal is disposed of;
  (b) the court will give the parties to that appeal notice of the day on which it will be heard; and
  (c) the party who gave the notice is not entitled to receive any costs of the separate hearing of that appeal unless the judge otherwise orders.

(4) Where no notice is given under sub-para. (3) within the period limited by that sub-paragraph:
  (a) the decision on the test-case appeal binds the parties to each of the other appeals;
  (b) without further hearing, the court will make, in each other appeal, an order similar to the order in the test-case appeal; and
  (c) the party to each other appeal who is in the same interest as the unsuccessful party to the selected appeal is liable for the costs of the test-case appeal in the same manner and to the same extent as the unsuccessful party to that appeal and an order directing him to pay such costs may be made and enforced accordingly.

(5) Sub-paragraph (4)(a) does not affect the right to appeal to the Court of Appeal of any party to an appeal other than the test-case appeal.

PD 54   Practice Direction—Judicial Review

As from 1 October 2007, a new para. 6.2 is inserted after para. 6.1:

6.2   Where the defendant or interested party to the claim for judicial review is the Asylum and Immigration Tribunal, the address for service of the claim form is the Asylum and Immigration Tribunal, Official Correspondence Unit, PO Box 6987, Leicester, LE1 6ZX or fax number (0116) 249 4131.

(Part 6 contains provisions about the service of claim forms.)

PD 55   Practice Direction—Possession Claims

As from 1 October 2007, para. 2.2 is replaced by:

2.2   Paragraphs 2.3 to 2.4B apply if the claim relates to residential property let on a tenancy.

A new para. 2.4B is inserted after para. 2.4A:

2.4B If the possession claim relies on a statutory ground or grounds for possession, the particulars of claim must specify the ground or grounds relied on.

Paragraph 10.1 is replaced by:

10.1 This paragraph applies where the court has made an order postponing the date for possession under the Housing Act 1985, s. 85(2)(b) (secure tenancies) or under the Housing Act 1988, s. 9(2)(b) (assured tenancies).

PD 55B   Practice Direction—Possession Claims Online

As from 1 October 2007, in para. 5.2, patient *is replaced by* protected party*, and a new para. 6.2A is inserted after para. 6.2:*

6.2A In the case of a possession claim for residential property that relies on a statutory ground or grounds for possession, the claimant must specify, in section 4(a) (or, if that is not possible, section 5) of the online claim form, the ground or grounds relied on.
(Paragraph 6.2A in its present form is intended only as a temporary expedient to overcome a limitation of the PCOL system. Action is in hand to modify the PCOL system to allow the information to be inserted in the online form in a more satisfactory way and it is intended that when that action is completed the paragraph will be suitably amended.)

Paragraph 6.3A is replaced by:

6.3A Paragraph 6.3B applies where the claimant has, before commencing proceedings, provided the defendant in schedule form with:
  (1) details of the dates and amounts of all payments due and payments made under the tenancy agreement, mortgage deed or mortgage account:
      (a) for a period of two years immediately preceding the date of commencing proceedings; or
      (b) if the first date of default occurred less than two years before that date, from the first date of default; and
  (2) a running total of the arrears.

In para. 6.3C(1), a full arrears history *is changed to* a full, up-to-date arrears history.

PD 57   Practice Direction—Probate

As from 1 October 2007, in para. 2.2, Caernarfon *and* Mold *are added to the list of Chancery district registries. In para. 3.2(2),* patient *is replaced by* protected party*. In para. 16(3),* patient within the meaning of r. 21.1(2) *is replaced by* a person who lacks capacity (within the meaning of the Mental Capacity Act 2005).

PD 59   Practice Direction—Mercantile Courts

As from 1 October 2007, in para. 1.2(1) Manchester and Newcastle *is changed to* Manchester, Mold and Newcastle upon Tyne.

PD 60   Practice Direction—Technology and Construction Court Claims

As from 1 October 2007, in para. 3.3, Newcastle, Nottingham and Salford *is changed to* Manchester, Mold, Newcastle upon Tyne and Nottingham. *In para. 3.4,* Newcastle, Nottingham and Salford *is changed to* Manchester, Mold, Newcastle upon Tyne and Nottingham.

PD 63   Practice Direction—Patents and Other Intellectual Property Claims

As from 1 October 2007, para. 18.2 is replaced by:

18.2   There are Chancery district registries at Birmingham, Bristol, Caernarfon, Cardiff, Leeds, Liverpool, Manchester, Mold, Newcastle upon Tyne and Preston.

CPR Part 65   Proceedings Relating to Anti-social Behaviour and Harassment

As from 1 October 2007, amendments are made by the Civil Procedure (Amendment) Rules 2007 (SI 2007/2204), r. 19. New paras (f) and (g) are inserted at the end of r. 65.1:

(f)   in Section VI, about applications for drinking banning orders and interim drinking banning orders under sections 4 and 9 of the Violent Crime Reduction Act 2006; and

(g)   in Section VII, about parenting orders under sections 26A and 26B of the Anti-social Behaviour Act 2003.

Rules 65.8, 65.9 and 65.10 are amended and the amended text is:

65.8   Scope of This Section and Interpretation

(1)   This Section applies to applications by local authorities under section 91(3) of the Anti-social Behaviour Act 2003 or under section 27(3) of the Police and Justice Act 2006 for a power of arrest to be attached to an injunction.
(Section 91 of the 2003 Act and section 27 of the 2006 Act apply to proceedings in which a local authority is a party by virtue of section 222 of the Local Government Act 1972 (power of local authority to bring, defend or appear in proceedings for the promotion or protection of the interests of inhabitants in their area))

(2)   In this Section 'the 2003 Act' means the Anti-social Behaviour Act 2003.

(3)   In this Section 'the 2006 Act' means the Police and Justice Act 2006.

65.9 Applications under Section 91(3) of the 2003 Act or section 27(3) of the 2006 Act for a Power of Arrest to Be Attached to Any Provision of an Injunction

(1) An application under section 91(3) of the 2003 Act or section 27(3) of the 2006 Act for a power of arrest to be attached to any provision of an injunction must be made in the proceedings seeking the injunction by—
    (a) the claim form;
    (b) the acknowledgment of service;
    (c) the defence or counterclaim in a Part 7 claim; or
    (d) application under Part 23.

(2) Every application must be supported by written evidence.

(3) Every application made on notice must be served personally, together with a copy of the written evidence, by the local authority on the person against whom the injunction is sought not less than 2 days before the hearing.

(Attention is drawn to rule 25.3(3)—applications without notice)

65.10 Injunction Containing Provisions to Which a Power of Arrest Is Attached

(1) Where a power of arrest is attached to a provision of an injunction on the application of a local authority under section 91(3) of the 2003 Act, the following rules in Section I of this Part shall apply—
    (a) rule 65.4; and
    (b) paragraphs (1), (2), (4) and (5) of rule 65.6.

(1A) Where a power of arrest is attached to a provision of an injunction on the application of a local authority under section 27(3) of the 2006 Act, the following rules in Section I of this Part apply—
    (a) rule 65.4;
    (b) paragraphs (1), (2), (4) and (5) of rule 65.6;
    (c) paragraph (1) of rule 65.7, as if the reference to paragraph 2(2)(b) of Schedule 15 to the Housing Act 1996 was a reference to paragraph 2(2)(b) of Schedule 10 to the 2006 Act; and
    (d) paragraph (2) of rule 65.7.

(2) CCR Order 29, rule 1 shall apply where an application is made in a county court to commit a person for breach of an injunction.

A new Section VII (rr. 65.37 to 65.41) is inserted after r. 65.36:

VII PARENTING ORDERS UNDER THE ANTI-SOCIAL BEHAVIOUR ACT 2003

65.37 Scope of This Section and Interpretation

(1) This Section of this Part applies in relation to applications for parenting orders under sections 26A and 26B of the Anti-social Behaviour Act 2003 by a relevant authority.

(2) In this Section—
    (a) 'the 2003 Act' means the Anti-social Behaviour Act 2003; and
    (b) 'relevant authority' has the same meaning as in section 26C of the 2003 Act.

65.38 Applications for Parenting Orders

(1) Subject to paragraph (2)—
    (a) where the relevant authority is the claimant in the proceedings, an application for an order under section 26A or 26B of the 2003 Act must be made in the claim form; and
    (b) where the relevant authority is a defendant in the proceedings, an application for such an order must be made by application notice which must be filed with the defence.

(2) Where the relevant authority becomes aware of the circumstances that lead it to apply for an order after its claim is issued or its defence filed, the application must be made by application notice as soon as possible thereafter.

(3) Where the application is made by application notice, it must normally be made on notice to the person against whom the order is sought.

65.39 Applications by the Relevant Authority to Be Joined to Proceedings

(1) Where the relevant authority is not a party to the proceedings—
    (a) an application under section 26C(2) of the 2003 Act to be made a party must be made in accordance with Section I of Part 19; and
    (b) the application to be made a party and the application for an order under section 26A or 26B of the 2003 Act must be made in the same application notice.
(2) The applications—
    (a) must be made as soon as possible after the relevant authority becomes aware of the proceedings; and
    (b) must normally be made on notice to the person against whom the order is sought.

65.40 Applications by the Relevant Authority to Join a Parent to Proceedings

(1) An application under section 26C(3) of the 2003 Act by a relevant authority which is a party to the proceedings to join a parent to those proceedings must be made—
    (a) in the same application notice as the application for an order under section 26A or 26B of the 2003 Act; and
    (b) as soon as possible after the relevant authority considers that the grounds for the application are met.
(2) Rule 19.2 does not apply in relation to an application made by a relevant authority under section 26C(3) of the 2003 Act to join a parent to the proceedings.
(3) The application notice must contain—
    (a) the relevant authority's reasons for claiming the anti-social behaviour of the child or young person is material in relation to the proceedings; and
    (b) details of the behaviour alleged.
(4) The application must normally be made on notice to the person against whom the order is sought.

65.41 Evidence

An application under section 26A, 26B or 26C of the 2003 Act must be accompanied by written evidence.

PD 65   Practice Direction—Anti-social Behaviour and Harassment

As from 1 October 2007, new paras 4A.1 and 4A.2 are inserted after para. 4.1:

Applications by Local Authorities for Power of Arrest to Be Attached to an Injunction

Application for bail under the 2006 Act

4A.1 The following paragraphs of Section I of this practice direction apply in relation to an application for bail by a person arrested under a power of arrest attached to an injunction under s. 27 of the 2006 Act:
    (1) para. 3.1(1), as if a reference to the Housing Act 1996, part V, ch. III, was a reference to s. 27 of the 2006 Act;
    (2) para. 3.2; and
    (3) para. 3.3.

Remand for medical examination and report

4A.2 Paragraph 4.1 of Section I of this practice direction applies in relation to s. 27 of the 2006 Act, as if a reference in para. 4.1 to the Housing Act 1996, s. 156(4), was a reference to s. 27(11) of the 2006 Act.

New paras 16.1 to 16.3 are inserted after para. 15.2:

VII PARENTING ORDERS UNDER THE ANTI-SOCIAL BEHAVIOUR ACT 2003

Applications for Parenting Orders

16.1 Where the applicant is a registered social landlord, the application must be supported by evidence that the relevant local authority has been consulted in accordance with s. 26B(8) of the 2003 Act.

16.2 An order under s. 26A or 26B of the 2003 Act must be served personally on the defendant.

16.3 An application by a relevant authority under s. 26C(3) of the 2003 Act to join a person to the proceedings may only be made against a person aged 18 or over.

PD 73   Practice Direction—Charging Orders, Stop Orders and Stop Notices

As from 1 October 2007, in the note following para. 4.2, Caernarfon and Mold are added to the list of Chancery district registries.

PD 74   Practice Direction—Enforcement of Judgments in Different Jurisdictions

As from 1 October 2007, para. 6.1 is replaced by:

6.1 Where a judgment is to be recognised and enforced in a Regulation State, the Judgments Regulation applies.

CPR Schedule 1

As from 1 October 2007, amendments are made by the Civil Procedure (Amendment) Rules 2007 (SI 2007/2204), r. 20. The following rules are revoked:

(a) RSC Order 93, rules 4, 5, 9, 10, 16, 17, 18 and 19;

(b) RSC Order 94, rules 4, 5, 8, 9, 12 and 13; and

(c) RSC Order 95, rules 1, 4, 5 and 6.

CPR Schedule 2

As from 1 October 2007, CCR, ord. 45, is revoked by the Civil Procedure (Amendment) Rules 2007 (SI 2007/2204), r. 20.

Practice Direction—Insolvency Proceedings

As from 1 October 2007, para. 17.8(b) is replaced by:

(b) 'Registrar of Appeals' means:
  (i) in relation to an appeal filed at the Royal Courts of Justice in London, a registrar in bankruptcy; and
  (ii) in relation to an appeal filed in a district registry, a district judge of that district registry.

Paragraph 17.10 is replaced by:

17.10 (1) An appeal from a decision of a registrar in bankruptcy must be filed at the Royal Courts of Justice in London.
  (2) An appeal from a decision of a district judge sitting in a district registry may be filed:
    (a) at the Royal Courts of Justice in London; or
    (b) in that district registry.
  (3) An appeal from a decision made in a county court may be filed:
    (a) at the Royal Courts of Justice in London; or
    (b) in the Chancery district registry for the area within which the county court exercises jurisdiction.
(There are Chancery district registries of the High Court at Birmingham, Bristol, Caernarfon, Cardiff, Leeds, Liverpool, Manchester, Mold, Newcastle upon Tyne and Preston. The county court districts that each district registry covers are set out in the Civil Courts Order 1983 (SI 1983/713), sch. 1.)

Paragraphs 17.22 and 17.23 are amended and the amended text is as follows:

17.22 The following practice applies to all first appeals to a judge of the High Court whether filed at the Royal Courts of Justice in London, or filed at one of the other venues referred to in para. 17.10 above:
  (1) on filing an appellant's notice in accordance with para. 17.11(2) above, the appellant must file:
    (a) two copies of the appeal notice for the use of the court, one of which must be stamped with the appropriate fee, and a number of additional copies equal to the number of persons who are to be served with it pursuant to para. 17.22(4) below;
    (aa) an approved transcript of the judgment of the lower court or, where there is no official record of the judgment, a document referred to in PD 52, para. 5.12.
    (b) a copy of the order under appeal; and
    (c) an estimate of time for the hearing.
  (2) The above documents may be lodged personally or by post and shall be lodged at the address of the appropriate venue listed below:
    (a) if the appeal is to be heard at the Royal Courts of Justice in London the documents must be lodged at Room 110, Thomas More Building, The Royal Courts of Justice, Strand, London WC2A 2LL;
    (b) if the appeal is to be heard in Birmingham, the documents must be lodged at the District Registry of the Chancery Division of the High Court, 33 Bull Street, Birmingham B4 6DS;
    (c) if the appeal is to be heard in Bristol the documents must be lodged at the District Registry of the Chancery Division of the High Court, Third Floor, Greyfriars, Lewins Mead, Bristol BS1 2NR;
    (ca) if the appeal is to be heard in Caernarfon the documents must be lodged at the District Registry of the Chancery Division of the High Court, Llanberis Road, Caernarfon, LL55 2DF;
    (d) if the appeal is to be heard in Cardiff the documents must be lodged at the District Registry of the Chancery Division of the High Court, First Floor, 2 Park Street, Cardiff CF10 1ET;

(e) if the appeal is to be heard in Leeds the documents must be lodged at the District Registry of the Chancery Division of the High Court, The Court House, 1 Oxford Row, Leeds LS1 3BG;

(f) if the appeal is to be heard in Liverpool the documents must be lodged at the District Registry of the Chancery Division of the High Court, Liverpool Combined Court Centre, Derby Square, Liverpool L2 1XA;

(g) if the appeal is to be heard in Manchester the documents must be lodged at the District Registry of the Chancery Division of the High Court, Courts of Justice, Crown Square, Manchester M60 9DJ;

(ga) if the appeal is to be heard in Mold the documents must be lodged at the District Registry of the Chancery Division of the High Court, Law Courts, Civic Centre, Mold, CH7 1AE;

(h) if the appeal is to be heard at Newcastle upon Tyne the documents must be lodged at the District Registry of the Chancery Division of the High Court, The Law Courts, Quayside, Newcastle upon Tyne NE1 3LA;

(i) if the appeal is to be heard in Preston the documents must be lodged at the District Registry of the Chancery Division of the High Court, The Combined Court Centre, Ringway, Preston PR1 2LL.

(3) If the documents are correct and in order the court at which the documents are filed will fix the appeal date and will also fix the place of hearing. That court will send letters to all the parties to the appeal informing them of the appeal date and of the place of hearing and indicating the time estimate given by the appellant. The parties will be invited to notify the court of any alternative or revised time estimates. In the absence of any such notification the estimate of the appellant will be taken as agreed. The court will also send to the appellant a document setting out the court's requirement concerning the form and content of the bundle of documents for the use of the judge. Not later than seven days before the appeal date the bundle of documents must be filed by the appellant at the address of the relevant venue as set out in para. 17.22(2) above and a copy of it must be served by the appellant on each respondent.

(4) The appeal notice must be served on all parties to the proceedings in the lower court who are directly affected by the appeal. This may include the official receiver, liquidator or trustee in bankruptcy.

(5) The appeal notice must be served by the appellant or by the legal representative of the appellant and may be effected by:
(a) any of the methods referred to in CPR, r. 6.2; or
(b) with permission of the court, an alternative method pursuant to CPR, r. 6.8.

(6) Service of an appeal notice shall be proved by a certificate of service in accordance with CPR, r. 6.10 (form N215) which must be filed at the relevant venue referred to at para. 17.22(2) above immediately after service.

(7) Subject to sub-paras (7A) and (7B), the appellant's notice must be accompanied by a skeleton argument and a written chronology of events relevant to the appeal. Alternatively, the skeleton argument and chronology may be included in the appellant's notice. Where the skeleton argument and chronology are so included they do not form part of the notice for the purposes of CPR, r. 52.8.

(7A) Where it is impracticable for the appellant's skeleton argument and chronology to accompany the appellant's notice they must be filed and served on all respondents within 14 days of filing the notice.

(7B) An appellant who is not represented need not file a skeleton argument nor a written chronology but is encouraged to do so since these documents may be helpful to the court.

(8) Where an appeal has been settled or where an appellant does not wish to continue with the appeal, the appeal may be disposed of on paper without a hearing. It may be dismissed by consent but the appeal court will not make an order allowing an appeal unless it is satisfied that the decision of the lower court was wrong. Any consent order signed by each party or letters of consent from each party must be lodged not later than 24 hours before the date fixed for the hearing of the appeal at the address of the appropriate venue as set out in para. 17.22(2) above and will be dealt with by the judge of the appeal court.

Attention is drawn to [PD 43–48, para. 13.4§] regarding costs where an order is made by consent without attendance.

17.23 Only the following paragraphs of PD 52, with any necessary modifications, shall apply to first appeals: 5.10 to 5.20.

Practice Direction—Directors Disqualification Proceedings

As from 1 October 2007, in paras 12.4(3) and 34.4(3), the list of Chancery district registries is changed to Birmingham, Bristol, Caernarfon, Cardiff, Leeds, Liverpool, Manchester, Mold, Newcastle upon Tyne, or Preston.

The following addresses are added to annex 1:

Caernarfon: The Chancery Listing Officer, The District Registry of the Chancery Division of the High Court, 1st Floor, Llanberis Road, Caernarfon, LL55 2DF.

Mold: The Chancery Listing Officer, The District Registry of the Chancery Division of the High Court, Law Courts, Civic Centre, Mold, CH7 1AE.

In annex 1, Newcastle *as the name of a district registry is changed to* Newcastle upon Tyne.

---

§ The text issued by the Ministry of Justice refers to an earlier version of the practice direction.

Supplement to Appendix 2
Pre-action Protocols

In the supplements to appendices 1 to 6 notes by the editors of *Blackstone's Civil Practice* are in italic type and the text of legislation is in upright type.

Pre-action Protocol for Housing Disrepair Cases

At the end of the third paragraph of the introduction, the reference to para. 4.1(a) *is corrected to* para. 4.1(b). *In para. 4.1(b), under the bullet point,* Other options in respect of the following specific categories (i) For council tenants, *the second paragraph of the bullet point,* The Right to Repair Scheme, *is replaced by:*

Information and leaflets about the scheme in England can be obtained from the Department for Communities and Local Government, Eland House, Bressenden Place, London SW1E 5DU. Tel: (020) 7944 3672. www.communities.gov.uk/index.asp?id=1152130.

Paragraph 4.1(f) is replaced by:

(f) The former Department for Transport, Local Government and the Regions issued *Good Practice Guidance on Housing Disrepair Legal Obligations* in January 2002. Copies of the Guidance (ISBN 185112523X) can be obtained from Communities and Local Government Publications, PO Box 236, Wetherby LS23 7NB. Tel: 0870 1226 236. Fax: 0870 1226 237. Textphone: 0870 1207 405. Email: communities@twoten.com. Free to download from the Communities and Local Government website at www.communities.gov.uk/index.asp?id=1502470. A summary, Housing Research Summary No. 154, is available free on the Communities and Local Government website at the following link www.communities.gov.uk/index.asp?id=1155697. Hard copies are no longer available. The Communities and Local Government website www.communities.gov.uk/index.asp?id=1150232 is a general source of information for landlords and tenants.

Paragraphs 4.2 to 4.10, which are printed correctly in Blackstone's Civil Practice 2008, *have now been restored to the text issued by the Ministry of Justice.*

Supplement to Appendix 5
Court Fees Orders

In the supplements to appendices 1 to 6 notes by the editors of *Blackstone's Civil Practice* are in italic type and the text of legislation is in upright type.

Civil Proceedings Fees Order 2004

Extensive amendments are made by the Civil Proceedings (Amendment) (No. 2) Order 2007 (SI 2007/2176) and the Civil Proceedings Fees (Amendment) (No. 2) (Amendment) Order 2007 (SI 2007/2801) as from 1 October 2007. The amended Order is:

Civil Proceedings Fees Order 2004
(SI 2004/3121)

The Lord Chancellor, in exercise of the powers conferred upon him by sections 92 and 108(6) of the Courts Act 2003, sections 414 and 415 of the Insolvency Act 1986, and section 128 of the Finance Act 1990, with the consent of the Treasury under section 92(1) of the Courts Act 2003 and after consultation with the Lord Chief Justice, the Master of the Rolls, the President of the Family Division, the Vice-Chancellor, the Head of Civil Justice and the Deputy Head of Civil Justice and the Civil Justice Council under section 92(5) and (6) of the Courts Act 2003 and with the sanction of the Treasury under sections 414(1) and 415(1) of the Insolvency Act 1986, hereby makes the following Order:

1 Citation, Commencement and Interpretation

(1) This Order may be cited as the Civil Proceedings Fees Order 2004 and shall come into force on the 4th January 2005.
(2) In this Order—
    (a) a fee referred to by number means the fee so numbered in Schedule 1 to this Order;
    (b) 'CCBC' means County Court Bulk Centre;
    (c) 'CPC' means Claim Production Centre;
    (d) 'the CPR' means the Civil Procedure Rules 1998;
    (e) expressions also used in the CPR have the same meaning as in those Rules;
    (f) 'family proceedings' means family proceedings in the High Court or in a county court as appropriate;
    (g) 'LSC' means the Legal Services Commission established under section 1 of the Access to Justice Act 1999;
    (h) 'Funding Code' means the code approved under section 9 of the Access to Justice Act 1999;
    (i) 'GLO' means a Group Litigation Order.

2 Fees to Be Taken

The fees set out in column 2 of Schedule 1 to this Order shall be taken in the Supreme Court and in county courts respectively in respect of the items described in column 1 in accordance with and subject to the directions specified in column 1.

3

The provisions of this Order shall not apply to—

(a) non-contentious probate business;
(b) [*revoked*]
(c) the enrolment of documents;
(d) criminal proceedings (except proceedings on the Crown side of the Queen's Bench Division to which the fees contained in Schedule 1 are applicable);
(e) proceedings by sheriffs, under-sheriffs, deputy-sheriffs or other officers of the sheriff; and
(f) family proceedings.

4 Remissions and Part Remissions

Schedule 1A applies for the purpose of ascertaining whether a party is entitled to the remission or part remission of a fee prescribed by this Order.

5

Where it appears to the Lord Chancellor that the payment of any fee prescribed by this Order would, owing to the exceptional circumstances of the particular case, involve undue financial hardship, he may reduce or remit the fee in that case.

6

(1) Subject to paragraph (2), where a fee has been paid at a time—
  (a) when, under article 4, it was not payable, the fee shall be refunded;
  (b) where the Lord Chancellor, if he had been aware of all the circumstances, would have reduced the fee under article 5, the amount by which the fee would have been reduced shall be refunded; and
  (c) where the Lord Chancellor, if he had been aware of all the circumstances, would have remitted the fee under article 5, the fee shall be refunded.
(2) No refund shall be made under paragraph (1) unless the party who paid the fee applies within 6 months of paying the fee.
(3) The Lord Chancellor may extend the period of 6 months referred to in paragraph (2) if he considers that there is good reason for an application being made after the end of the period of 6 months.

7

Where by any convention entered into by Her Majesty with any foreign power it is provided that no fee shall be required to be paid in respect of any proceedings, the fees specified in this Order shall not be taken in respect of those proceedings.

8 Revocations

The Orders specified in Schedule 2, in so far as they were made under sections 414 and 415 of the Insolvency Act 1986 and section 128 of the Finance Act 1990, shall be revoked.

SCHEDULE 1   FEES TO BE TAKEN

[Schedule introduced by art. 2]

Column 1 *Number and description of fee*	Column 2 *Amount of fee*
1 Starting proceedings (High Court and county court)	
1.1 On starting proceedings (including proceedings issued after permission to issue is granted but excluding CPC cases brought by Centre users or cases brought by Money Claim OnLine users) to recover a sum of money where the sum claimed:	
(a) does not exceed £300	£30
(b) exceeds £300 but does not exceed £500	£45
(c) exceeds £500 but does not exceed £1,000	£65
(d) exceeds £1,000 but does not exceed £1,500	£75
(e) exceeds £1,500 but does not exceed £3,000	£85
(f) exceeds £3,000 but does not exceed £5,000	£108

Column 1 Number and description of fee	Column 2 Amount of fee
(g) exceeds £5,000 but does not exceed £15,000	£225
(h) exceeds £15,000 but does not exceed £50,000	£360
(i) exceeds £50,000 but does not exceed £100,000	£630
(j) exceeds £100,000 but does not exceed £150,000	£810
(k) exceeds £150,000 but does not exceed £200,000	£990
(l) exceeds £200,000 but does not exceed £250,000	£1,170
(m) exceeds £250,000 but does not exceed £300,000	£1,350
(n) exceeds £300,000 or is not limited	£1,530

1.2 On starting proceedings to recover a sum of money in Claim Production Centre cases brought by Centre users, where the sum claimed:

(a) does not exceed £300	£15
(b) exceeds £300 but does not exceed £500	£30
(c) exceeds £500 but does not exceed £1,000	£55
(d) exceeds £1,000 but does not exceed £1,500	£65
(e) exceeds £1,500 but does not exceed £3,000	£75
(f) exceeds £3,000 but does not exceed £5,000	£85
(g) exceeds £5,000 but does not exceed £15,000	£190
(h) exceeds £15,000 but does not exceed £50,000	£310
(i) exceeds £50,000 but does not exceed £100,000	£550

1.3 On starting proceedings to recover a sum of money brought by Money Claim OnLine users where the sum claimed:

(a) does not exceed £300	£25
(b) exceeds £300 but does not exceed £500	£35
(c) exceeds £500 but does not exceed £1,000	£60
(d) exceeds £1,000 but does not exceed £1,500	£70
(e) exceeds £1,500 but does not exceed £3,000	£80
(f) exceeds £3,000 but does not exceed £5,000	£100
(g) exceeds £5,000 but does not exceed £15,000	£210
(h) exceeds £15,000 but does not exceed £50,000	£340
(i) exceeds £50,000 but does not exceed £100,000	£595

Fees 1.1, 1.2 and 1.3
Where the claimant is making a claim for interest on a specified sum of money, the amount on which the fee is calculated is the total amount of the claim and the interest.

1.4 On starting proceedings for the recovery of land in the county court brought by Possession Claim OnLine users	£100

1.5 On starting proceedings for any other remedy (including proceedings issued after permission to issue is granted)—

— in the High Court	£400
— in the county court	£150

Fees 1.1, 1.4 and 1.5. Recovery of land or goods
Where a claim for money is additional or alternative to a claim for recovery of land or goods, only fee 1.4 or 1.5 shall be payable.

Fees 1.1 and 1.5. Claims other than recovery of land or goods
Where a claim for money is additional to a non money claim (other than a claim for recovery of land or goods), then fee 1.1 is payable in addition to fee 1.5.
Where a claim for money is alternative to a non money claim (other than a claim for recovery of land or goods), only fee 1.1 shall be payable in the High Court, and, in the county court, fee 1.1 or fee 1.5 shall be payable, whichever is the greater.

Fees 1.1 and 1.5
Where more than one non money claim is made in the same proceedings, fee 1.5 shall be payable once only, in addition to any fee which may be payable under fee 1.1.

Fees 1.1 and 1.5 shall not be payable where fee 1.8(b), fee 1.9(a), fee 10.1 or fee 3 apply.

Column 1 *Number and description of fee*	Column 2 *Amount of fee*

Fees 1.1 and 1.5. Amendment of claim or counterclaim
Where the claim or counterclaim is amended, and the fee paid before amendment is less than that which would have been payable if the document, as amended, had been so drawn in the first instance, the party amending the document shall pay the difference.

1.6 On the filing of proceedings against a party or parties not named in the proceedings £40
Fee 1.6
Fee 1.6 shall be payable by a defendant who adds or substitutes a party or parties to the proceedings or by a claimant who adds or substitutes a defendant or defendants.

1.7 On the filing of a counterclaim The same fee as if the remedy sought were the subject of separate proceedings
Fee 1.7
No fee is payable on a counterclaim which a defendant is required to make under the CPR because he contends that he has any claim or is entitled to any remedy relating to a grant of probate of a will, or letters of administration of an estate, of a deceased person.

1.8 (a) On an application for permission to issue proceedings £40
(b) On an application for an order under Part III of the Solicitors Act 1974 for the assessment of costs payable to a solicitor by his client or on starting costs-only proceedings £40

1.9(a) On starting proceedings for judicial review £50
Where the court has made an order giving permission to proceed with a claim for judicial review, there shall be payable by the claimant within 7 days of service on the claimant of that order:
1.9(b) if the judicial review procedure has been started £180
1.9(c) if the claim for judicial review was started otherwise than by using the judicial review procedure £50

2 General Fees (High Court and county court)
2.1 On the claimant filing an allocation questionnaire; or
— where the court dispenses with the need for an allocation questionnaire, within 14 days of the date of despatch of the notice of allocation to track; or
— where the CPR or a Practice Direction provide for automatic allocation or provide that the rules on allocation shall not apply, within 28 days of the filing of the defence (or the filing of the last defence if there is more than one defendant), or within 28 days of the expiry of the time permitted for filing all defences if sooner:
(a) if the case is on the small claims track and the claim exceeds £1,500 £35
(b) if the case is on the fast track or multi-track £200

Fee 2.1
Fee 2.1 shall be payable by the claimant except where the action is proceeding on the counterclaim alone, when it shall be payable by the defendant—
— on the defendant filing an allocation questionnaire; or
— where the court dispenses with the need for an allocation questionnaire, within 14 days of the date of despatch of the notice of allocation to track; or
— where the CPR or a Practice Direction provide for automatic allocation or provide that the rules on allocation shall not apply, within 28 days of the filing of the defence to the counterclaim (or the filing of the last defence to the counterclaim if there is more than one party entitled to file a defence to the counterclaim), or within 28 days of the expiry of the time permitted for filing all defences to the counterclaim if sooner.
Where fee 2.1 is payable on the filing of an allocation questionnaire, by the claimant or the defendant as the case may be, the fee payable shall be based on the track for the case specified in the allocation questionnaire. If the case is subsequently allocated to a track which attracts a higher fee then the difference in fee shall be payable, by the party liable to pay the fee, within 14 days of the date of despatch of notice of allocation to track. If the case is allocated to a track which attracts a lower fee the difference in fee shall be refunded.

Column 1 Number and description of fee	Column 2 Amount of fee

2.2 On the claimant filing a listing questionnaire; or where the court fixes the trial date or trial week without the need for a listing questionnaire, within 14 days of the date of despatch of the notice (or the date when oral notice is given if no written notice is given) of the trial week or the trial date if no trial week is fixed.   £100

Fee 2.2
Fee 2.2 shall be payable by the claimant except where the action is proceeding on the counterclaim alone, when it shall be payable by the defendant—
— on the defendant filing a listing questionnaire; or
— where the court fixes the trial date or trial week without the need for a listing questionnaire, within 14 days of the date of despatch of the notice (or the date when oral notice is given if no written notice is given) of the trial week or the trial date if no trial week is fixed.

Fees 2.1 and 2.2 in the High Court and the county court
Fees 2.1 and 2.2 shall be payable as appropriate where the court allocates a case to track for a trial of the assessment of damages.
Fees 2.1 and 2.2 shall not be payable in relation to claims managed under a GLO after that GLO is made.
Fees 2.1 and 2.2 shall be payable once only in the same proceedings.
Fee 2.1 shall not be payable where the procedure in Part 8 of the CPR is used.
Fee 2.2 shall not be payable where the court fixed the hearing date on the issue of the claim.

Fees 2.1 and 2.2 in the county court
Fee 2.1 shall not be payable in proceedings where the only claim is a claim to recover a sum of money and the sum claimed does not exceed £1,500.
Fee 2.2 shall not be payable in respect of a case on the small claims track

2.3 On the occasion of fee 2.2 becoming payable; or where the claim is on the small claims track, within 14 days of the date of despatch of the notice (or the date when oral notice is given if no written notice is given) of the trial week or the trial date if no trial week is fixed a fee payable for the hearing of:

(a) a case on the multi-track	£1,000
(b) a case on the fast track £100	£500
(c) a case on the small claims track where the sum claimed:	
(i) does not exceed £300	£25
(ii) exceeds £300 but does not exceed £500	£50
(iii) exceeds £500 but does not exceed £1,000	£75
(iv) exceeds £1,000 but does not exceed £1,500	£100
(v) exceeds £1,500 but does not exceed £3,000	£150
(vi) exceeds £3,000 but does not exceed £5,000	£300

Fee 2.3
Fee 2.3 shall be payable by the claimant except where the action is proceeding on the counterclaim alone, when it shall be payable by the defendant—
— on the defendant filing a listing questionnaire; or
— where the claim is on the small claims track or the court fixes the trial date or trial week without the need for a listing questionnaire, within 14 days of the date of despatch of the notice (or the date when oral notice is given if no written notice is given) of the trial week or the trial date if no trial week is fixed.
Where a case is on the multi-track or fast track and, after a hearing date has been fixed, the court receives notice in writing from the party who paid the hearing fee that the case has been settled or discontinued then the following percentages of the hearing fee shall be refunded—
(i)   100% if the court is notified more than 28 days before the hearing;
(ii)   75% if the court is notified between 14 and 28 days before the hearing;
(iii)   50% if the court is notified between 7 and 14 days before the hearing.
Where a case is on the small claims track and, after a hearing date has been fixed, the court receives notice in writing from the party who paid the hearing fee, at least 7 days before the date set for the hearing, that the case has been settled or discontinued the hearing fee shall be refunded in full.

Column 1 Number and description of fee	Column 2 Amount of fee

Fee 2.3 shall not be payable in respect of a case where the court fixed the hearing date on the issue of the claim.

2.4 In the High Court on filing—
— an appellant's notice, or
— a respondent's notice where the respondent is appealing or wishes to ask the appeal court to uphold the order of the lower court for reasons different from or additional to those given by the lower court
£200

2.5 In the county court on filing—
— an appellant's notice, or
— a respondent's notice where the respondent is appealing or wishes to ask the appeal court to uphold the order of the lower court for reasons different from or additional to those given by the lower court:
(a) in a claim allocated to the small claims track   £100
(b) in all other claims   £120

Fees 2.4 and 2.5
Fees 2.4 and 2.5 do not apply on appeals against a decision made in detailed assessment proceedings.

2.6 On an application on notice where no other fee is specified   £75

2.7 On an application by consent or without notice for a judgment or order where no other fee is specified   £40
For the purpose of fee 2.7 a request for a judgment or order on admission or in default shall not constitute an application and no fee shall be payable.

Fee 2.7 shall not be payable in relation to an application by consent for an adjournment of a hearing where the application is received by the court at least 14 days before the date set for that hearing.

Fees 2.6 and 2.7
Fees 2.6 and 2.7 shall not be payable when an application is made in an appeal notice or is filed at the same time as an appeal notice.

2.8 On an application for a summons or order for a witness to attend court to be examined on oath or an order for evidence to be taken by deposition, other than an application for which fee 7.2 or 8.3 is payable   £35

2.9 On an application to vary a judgment or suspend enforcement (where more than one remedy is sought in the same application only one fee shall be payable)   £35

2.10 Register of judgments kept under section 98 of the Courts Act 2003—
On a request for the issue of a certificate of satisfaction   £15

3 Companies Act 1985 and Insolvency Act 1986 (High Court and county court)

3.1 On entering a bankruptcy petition:
(a) if presented by a debtor or the personal representative of a deceased debtor   £150
(b) if presented by a creditor or other person   £190

3.2 On entering a petition for an administration order   £150

3.3 On entering any other petition   £190
One fee only is payable where more than one petition is presented in relation to a partnership.

3.4(a) On a request for a certificate of discharge from bankruptcy   £60
**   (b) and after the first certificate, for each copy**   £5

3.5 On an application under the Companies Act 1985 or the Insolvency Act 1986 other than one brought by petition and where no other fee is specified   £130

Fee 3.5
Fee 3.5 is not payable where the application is made in existing proceedings.

Column 1 *Number and description of fee*	*Column 2* *Amount of fee*
3.6 On an application for the conversion of a voluntary arrangement into a winding up or bankruptcy under Article 37 of Council Regulation (EC) No. 1346/2000	£130
3.7 On an application, for the purposes of Council Regulation (EC) No. 1346/2000, for an order confirming creditors' voluntary winding up (where the company has passed a resolution for voluntary winding up, and no declaration under section 89 of the Insolvency Act 1986 has been made)	£30
3.8 On filing— — a notice of intention to appoint an administrator under paragraph 14 of Schedule B1 to the Insolvency Act 1986 or in accordance with paragraph 27 of that Schedule; or — a notice of appointment of an administrator in accordance with paragraphs 18 or 29 of that Schedule	£30
Fee 3.8 Where a person pays fee 3.8 on filing a notice of intention to appoint an administrator, no fee shall be payable on that same person filing a notice of appointment of that administrator.	
3.9 On submitting a nominee's report under section 2(2) of the Insolvency Act 1986	£30
3.10 On filing documents in accordance with paragraph 7(1) of Schedule A1 to the Insolvency Act 1986	£30
3.11 On an application by consent or without notice within existing proceedings where no other fee is specified	£30
3.12 On an application with notice within existing proceedings where no other fee is specified	£30
3.13 On a search in person of the bankruptcy and companies records, in a county court	£40
Requests and applications with no fee. No fee is payable on a request or on an application to the Court by the Official Receiver when applying only in the capacity of Official Receiver to the case (and not as trustee or liquidator), or on an application to set aside a statutory demand.	
4 Copy Documents (Court of Appeal, High Court and county court) **4.1 On a request for a copy of a document** (other than where fee 4.2 applies): (a) for ten pages or less (b) for each subsequent page	 £5 50p
Fee 4.1 Fee 4.1 shall be payable for a faxed copy or for examining a plain copy and marking it as an examined copy and shall be payable whether or not the copy is issued as an office copy.	
4.2 On a request for a copy of a document on a computer disk or in other electronic form, for each such copy	£5
5 Determination of costs (Supreme Court and county court). Fee 5 does not apply to the determination in the Supreme Court of costs incurred in the Court of Protection.	
5.1 On the filing of a request for detailed assessment where the party filing the request is legally aided or is funded by the LSC and no other party is ordered to pay the costs of the proceedings— — in the Supreme Court — in the county court	 £120 £105
5.2 On the filing of a request for detailed assessment in any case where fee 5.1 does not apply; or on the filing of a request for a hearing date for the assessment of costs payable to a solicitor by his client pursuant to an order under Part III of the Solicitors Act 1974 where the amount of the costs to be assessed: (a) does not exceed £15,000 (b) exceeds £15,000 but does not exceed £50,000 (c) exceeds £50,000 but does not exceed £100,000 (d) exceeds £100,000 but does not exceed £150,000 (e) exceeds £150,000 but does not exceed £200,000	 £300 £600 £900 £1,200 £1,500

Column 1 *Number and description of fee*	Column 2 *Amount of fee*
(f) exceeds £200,000 but does not exceed £300,000	£2,250
(g) exceeds £300,000 but does not exceed £500,000	£3,750
(h) exceeds £500,000	£5,000

Where there is a combined party and party and legal aid, or a combined party and party and LSC, or a combined party and party, legal aid and LSC determination of costs, fee 5.2 shall be attributed proportionately to the party and party, legal aid, or LSC (as the case may be) portions of the bill on the basis of the amount allowed.

5.3 On a request for the issue of a default costs certificate—	
— in the Supreme Court	£50
— in the county court	£45
5.4 On an appeal against a decision made in detailed assessment proceedings—	
— in the Supreme Court	£200
— in the county court	£105
5.5 On applying for the court's approval of a certificate of costs payable from the Community Legal Service Fund—	
— in the Supreme Court	£50
— in the county court	£35

Fee 5.5
Fee 5.5 is payable at the time of applying for the court's approval and is recoverable only against the Community Legal Service Fund.

5.6 On a request or application to set aside a default costs certificate—	
— in the Supreme Court	£100
— in the county court	£65

6 Determination in the Supreme Court of costs incurred in the Court of Protection

6.1 On the filing of a request for detailed assessment:	
(a) where the amount of the costs to be assessed (excluding VAT and disbursements) does not exceed £3,000	£100
(b) in all other cases	£200
6.2 On an appeal against a decision made in detailed assessment proceedings	£60
6.3 On a request or application to set aside a default costs certificate	£60

7 Enforcement in the High Court

7.1 On sealing a writ of execution/possession/delivery	£50

Where the recovery of a sum of money is sought in addition to a writ of possession and delivery, no further fee is payable.

7.2 On an application for an order requiring a judgment debtor or other person to attend court to provide information in connection with enforcement of a judgment or order	£50
7.3 (a) On an application for a third party debt order or the appointment of a receiver by way of equitable execution	£100
(b) On an application for a charging order	£100

Fee 7.3(a) and (b)
Fee 7.3(a) shall be payable in respect of each third party against whom the order is sought.
Fee 7.3(b) shall be payable in respect of each application issued.

7.4 On an application for a judgment summons	£100
7.5 On a request or application to register a judgment or order, or for permission to enforce an arbitration award, or for a certificate or a certified copy of a judgment or order for use abroad	£50

8 Enforcement in the county court

8.1 On an application for or in relation to enforcement of a judgment or order of a county court or through a county court—

Column 1 *Number and description of fee*	*Column 2* *Amount of fee*
In cases other than CCBC cases brought by Centre users, by the issue of a warrant of execution against goods except a warrant to enforce payment of a fine:	
(a) Where the amount for which the warrant issues does not exceed £125	£35
(b) Where the amount for which the warrant issues exceeds £125	£55
In CCBC cases brought by Centre users, by the issue of a warrant of execution against goods except a warrant to enforce payment of a fine:	
(a) Where the amount for which the warrant issues does not exceed £125	£25
(b) Where the amount for which the warrant issues exceeds £125	£45
8.2 On a request for a further attempt at execution of a warrant at a new address following a notice of the reason for non-execution (except a further attempt following suspension and CCBC cases brought by Centre users)	£25
8.3 On an application for an order requiring a judgment debtor or other person to attend court to provide information in connection with enforcement of a judgment or order	£45
8.4(a) On an application for a third party debt order or the appointment of a receiver by way of equitable execution	£55
(b) On an application for a charging order	£55
Fee 8.4(a) and (b) Fee 8.4(a) shall be payable in respect of each third party against whom the order is sought. Fee 8.4(b) shall be payable in respect of each application issued.	
8.5 On an application for a judgment summons	£95
8.6 On the issue of a warrant of possession or a warrant of delivery Where the recovery of a sum of money is sought in addition, no further fee is payable.	£95
8.7 On an application for an attachment of earnings order (other than a consolidated attachment of earnings order) to secure payment of a judgment debt	£65
Fee 8.7 Fee 8.7 is payable for each defendant against whom an order is sought. Fee 8.7 is not payable where the attachment of earnings order is made on the hearing of a judgment summons.	
8.8 On a consolidated attachment of earnings order or on an administration order	For every £1 or part of a £1 of the money paid into court in respect of debts due to creditors—10p
Fee 8.8 Fee 8.8 shall be calculated on any money paid into court under any order at the rate in force at the time when the order was made (or, where the order has been amended, at the time of the last amendment before the date of payment).	
8.9 On the application for the recovery of a tribunal award	£35
8.10 On a request for an order to recover a sum that is—	£5
— a specified debt within the meaning of the Enforcement of Road Traffic Debts Order 1993 as amended from time to time; or	
— pursuant to an enactment, treated as a specified debt for the purposes of that Order	
No fee is payable on—	
— an application for an extension of time to serve a statutory declaration in connection with any such order; or	
— a request to issue a warrant of execution to enforce any such order.	

Column 1 *Number and description of fee*	*Column 2* *Amount of fee*
9 Sale (county court only)	
9.1 For removing or taking steps to remove goods to a place of deposit	The reasonable expenses incurred
Fee 9.1 is to include the reasonable expenses of feeding and caring for any animals.	
9.2 For advertising a sale by public auction pursuant to section 97 of the County Courts Act 1984	The reasonable expenses incurred
9.3 For the appraisement of goods	5p in the £1 or part of a £1 of the appraised value
9.4 For the sale of goods (including advertisements, catalogues, sale and commission and delivery of goods)	15p in the £1 or part of a £1 on the amount realised by the sale or such other sum as the district judge may consider to be justified in the circumstances
9.5 Where no sale takes place by reason of an execution being withdrawn, satisfied or stopped	(a) 10p in the £1 or part of a £1 on the value of the goods seized, the value to be the appraised value where the goods have been appraised or such other sum as the district judge may consider to be justified in the circumstances; and in addition (b) any sum payable under fee 9.1, 9.2 or 9.3

FEES PAYABLE IN HIGH COURT ONLY

10 Miscellaneous proceedings or matters

Bills of Sale

10.1 On filing any document under the Bills of Sale Acts 1878 and the Bills of Sale Act (1878) Amendment Act 1882 or on an application under section 15 of the Bills of Sale Act 1878 for an order that a memorandum of satisfaction be written on a registered copy of the bill	£25

Column 1 *Number and description of fee*	*Column 2* *Amount of fee*

Searches

10.2 For an official certificate of the result of a search for each name, in any register or index held by the court; or in the Court Funds Office, for an official certificate of the result of a search of unclaimed balances for a specified period of up to 50 years — £40

10.3 On a search in person of the bankruptcy and companies records, including inspection, for each 15 minutes or part of 15 minutes — £5

Judge sitting as arbitrator

10.4 On the appointment of:
(a) a judge of the Commercial Court as an arbitrator or umpire under section 93 of the Arbitration Act 1996; or — £1,800
(b) a judge of the Technology and Construction Court as an arbitrator or umpire under section 93 of the Arbitration Act 1996 — £1,400

10.5 For every day or part of a day (after the first day) of the hearing before:
(a) a judge of the Commercial Court; or — £1,800
(b) a judge of the Technology and Construction Court, so appointed as arbitrator or umpire — £1,400

Where fee 10.4 has been paid on the appointment of a judge of the Commercial Court or a judge of the Technology and Construction Court as an arbitrator or umpire but the arbitration does not proceed to a hearing or an award, the fee shall be refunded.

11 Fees payable in Admiralty matters
In the Admiralty Registrar and Marshal's Office—

11.1 On the issue of a warrant for the arrest of a ship or goods — £200

11.2 On the sale of a ship or goods—
Subject to a minimum fee of £200:
(a) for every £100 or fraction of £100 of the price up to £100,000 — £1
(b) for every £100 or fraction of £100 of the price exceeding £100,000 — 50p
Where there is sufficient proceeds of sale in court, fee 11.2 shall be taken by transfer from the proceeds of sale in court.

11.3 On entering a reference for hearing by the Registrar — £50

FEES PAYABLE IN HIGH COURT AND COURT OF APPEAL ONLY

12 Affidavits
12.1 On taking an affidavit or an affirmation or attestation upon honour in lieu of an affidavit or a declaration except for the purpose of receipt of dividends from the Accountant General and for a declaration by a shorthand writer appointed in insolvency proceedings—
— for each person making any of the above — £10

12.2 For each exhibit referred to in an affidavit, affirmation, attestation or declaration for which fee 12.1 is payable — £2

FEES PAYABLE IN COURT OF APPEAL ONLY

13 Fees payable in appeals to the Court of Appeal
13.1(a) Where in an appeal notice permission to appeal or an extension of time for appealing is applied for (or both are applied for)— — £200
    — on filing an appellant's notice, or
    — where the respondent is appealing, on filing a respondent's notice
13.1(b) Where permission to appeal is not required or has been granted by the lower court— — £400
    — on filing an appellant's notice, or
    — on filing a respondent's notice where the respondent is appealing
13.1(c) On the appellant filing an appeal questionnaire (unless the appellant has paid fee 13.1(b), or on the respondent filing an appeal questionnaire (unless the respondent has paid fee 13.1(b)) — £400

Column 1 *Number and description of fee*	*Column 2* *Amount of fee*
13.2 On filing a respondent's notice where the respondent wishes to ask the appeal court to uphold the order of the lower court for reasons different from or additional to those given by the lower court	£200
13.3 On filing an application notice Fee 13.3 Fee 13.3 shall not be payable for an application made in an appeal notice.	£200

SCHEDULE 1A   REMISSION AND PART REMISSION OF FEES

[Schedule introduced by art. 4]

Interpretation

1.—(1) In this Schedule—

'child care costs' and 'the Independent Living Funds' have the meaning given to them in the Criminal Defence Service (Financial Eligibility) Regulations 2006;

'child' means a child of the party, living in his household, under the age of 18;

'couple' has the meaning given in section 3(5A) of the Tax Credits Act 2002;

'disposable monthly income' has the meaning given in paragraph 5;

'excluded benefits' means—

    (a) any of the following benefits payable under the Social Security Contributions and Benefits Act 1992—

        (i) attendance allowance paid under section 64;

        (ii) severe disablement allowance;

        (iii) carer's allowance;

        (iv) disability living allowance;

        (v) constant attendance allowance paid under section 104 or paragraph 4 or 7(2) of Schedule 8 as an increase to a disablement pension;

        (vi) council tax benefit;

        (vii) any payment made out of the social fund;

        (viii) housing benefit;

    (b) any direct payments made under the Community Care, Services for Carers and Children's Services (Direct Payments) (England) Regulations 2003 or the Community Care, Services for Carers and Children's Services (Direct Payments) (Wales) Regulations 2004;

    (c) a back to work bonus payable under section 626 of the Jobseekers Act 1995;

    (d) any exceptionally severe disablement allowance paid under the Personal Injuries (Civilians) Scheme 1983;

    (e) any pensions paid under the Naval, Military and Air Forces etc (Disablement and Death) Service Pension Order 2006;

    (f) any payments made from the Independent Living Funds; and

    (g) any financial support paid under an agreement for the care of a foster child;

        'gross annual income' means total annual income, for the 12 months preceding the application for remission or part remission, from all sources other than receipt of any of the excluded benefits;

        'gross monthly income' means total monthly income, for the month in which the application for remission or part remission is made, from all sources other than receipt of any of the excluded benefits;

        'partner' means a person with whom the party lives as a couple and includes a person with whom the party is not currently living but from whom he is not living separate and apart;

'party' means the party who would, but for this Schedule, be liable to pay the fee required under this Order; and

'restraint order' means—

(a) an order under section 42(1A) of the Supreme Court Act 1981; or

(b) a civil restraint order under rule 3.11 of the Civil Procedure Rules 1998 or a practice direction made under that rule.

(2) Paragraphs 2, 3 and 4 are subject to the provisions of paragraphs 8 (vexatious litigants) and 9 (exception).

Full Remission of Fees—Qualifying Benefits

2.—(1) No fee shall be payable under this Order by a party who, at the time when a fee would otherwise be payable—

(a) is in receipt of a qualifying benefit; and

(b) is not in receipt of, as appropriate, either—

(i) representation under Part IV of the Legal Aid Act 1988 for the purposes of the proceedings; or

(ii) funding provided by the LSC for the purposes of the proceedings and for which a certificate has been issued under the Funding Code certifying a decision to fund services for that party.

(2) The following are qualifying benefits for the purposes of paragraph (1)(a)—

(a) income support under the Social Security Contributions and Benefits Act 1992;

(b) working tax credit, provided that no child tax credit is being paid to the party;

(c) income-based jobseeker's allowance under the Jobseekers Act 1995; and

(d) guarantee credit under the State Pension Credit Act 2002.

Full remission of Fees—Gross Annual Income

3.—(1) No fee shall be payable under this Order by a party if, at the time when the fee would otherwise be payable, he has the number of children specified in column 1 of the table below and—

(a) if he is single, his gross annual income does not exceed the amount set out in the appropriate row of column 2; or

(b) if he is one of a couple, the gross annual income of the couple does not exceed the amount set out in the appropriate row of column 3.

Column 1 Number of children of party paying fee	Column 2 Single	Column 3 Couple
no children	£12,000	£16,000
1 child	£14,470	£18,470
2 children	£16,940	£20,940
3 children	£19,410	£23,410
4 children	£21,880	£25,880

(2) If the party paying the fee has more than 4 children then the relevant amount of gross annual income shall be the amount specified in the table for 4 children plus the sum of £2,470 for each additional child.

Full and Part Remission of Fees—Disposable Monthly Income

4.—(1) No fee shall be payable under this Order by a party if, at the time when the fee would otherwise be payable, his disposable monthly income is £50 or less.

(2) The maximum amount of fee payable by a party is—

(a) if his disposable monthly income is more than £50 but does not exceed £210, an amount equal to one-quarter of every £10 of his disposable monthly income up to a maximum of £50; and

(b) if his disposable monthly income is more than £210, an amount equal to £50 plus one-half of every £10 over £200 of his disposable monthly income.

(3) Where the fee that would otherwise be payable under this Order is greater than the maximum fee which a party is required to pay as calculated in sub-paragraph (2), the fee shall be remitted to the amount payable under that sub-paragraph.

Disposable Monthly Income

5.—(1) A party's disposable monthly income is his gross monthly income for the month in which the fee becomes payable ('the period') less the deductions referred to in subparagraphs (2) and (3).

(2) There shall be deducted from the gross monthly income—
   (a) income tax paid or payable in respect of the period;
   (b) any contributions estimated to have been paid under Part I of the Social Security Contributions and Benefits Act 1992;
   (c) either—
      (i) monthly rent or monthly payment in respect of a mortgage debt or hereditable security, payable by him in respect of his only or main dwelling, less any housing benefit paid under the Social Security Contributions and Benefits Act 1992; or
      (ii) the monthly cost of his living accommodation;
   (d) any child care costs paid or payable in respect of the period;
   (e) if the party is making bona fide payments for the maintenance of a child who is not a member of his household, the amount of such payments paid or payable in respect of the period;
   (f) any amount paid or payable by the party, in respect of the period, in pursuance of a court order.

(3) There shall be deducted from the gross monthly income an amount representing the cost of living expenses in respect of the period being—
   (a) £279; plus
   (b) £198 for each child of the party; plus
   (c) £142, if the party has a partner.

Resources of Partners

6.—(1) For the purpose of determining whether a party is entitled to the remission or part remission of a fee in accordance with this Schedule, the income of his partner, if any, is to be included as income of the party.

(2) The receipt by a partner of a qualifying benefit does not entitle a party to remission of a fee.

Application for Remission or Part Remission of Fees

7.—(1) An application for remission or part remission of a fee shall be made to the court officer at the time when the fee would otherwise be payable.

(2) If the applicant is claiming a full remission of fees he must provide documentary evidence of, as the case may be—
   (a) his entitlement to a qualifying benefit; or
   (b) his gross annual income and, if applicable, the children included for the purposes of paragraph 3.

(3) If the applicant is claiming a full or part remission of fees under paragraph 4, he must provide documentary evidence of—
   (a) such of his gross monthly income as he derives from—
      (i) employment;
      (ii) rental or other income received from persons living with him by reason of their residence in his home;
      (iii) a pension; or
      (iv) a state benefit, not being an excluded benefit;
   (b) any expenditure being deducted from his gross monthly income in accordance with paragraph 5(2).

Vexatious Litigants

8.—(1) This paragraph applies where—
    (a) a restraint order is in force against a party;
    (b) the party makes an application for leave to—
        (i) issue proceedings or take a step in proceedings as required by the restraint order;
        (ii) apply for amendment or discharge of the order; or
        (iii) appeal the order.
(2) The fee prescribed for the application by Schedule 1 to this Order shall be payable in full.
(3) If the court grants the permission requested there shall be refunded to the applicant the difference between—
    (a) the fee paid; and
    (b) the fee that would have been payable if this Schedule had been applied without reference to this paragraph.

Exception

9. This Schedule does not apply to fee 8.8 (fee payable on a consolidated attachment of earnings order or an administration order).

SCHEDULE 2   ORDERS REVOKED

[Schedule introduced by art. 8]

Title	Reference
The Supreme Court Fees Order 1999	S.I. 1999/687
The Supreme Court Fees (Amendment) Order 1999	S.I. 1999/2569
The Supreme Court Fees (Amendment) Order 2000	S.I. 2000/641
The Supreme Court Fees (Amendment) Order 2003	S.I. 2003/646
The Supreme Court Fees (Amendment) Order 2004	S.I. 2004/2100
The Supreme Court Fees (Amendment No. 2) Order 2000	S.I. 2000/937
The Supreme Court Fees (Amendment No. 2) Order 2003	S.I. 2003/717
The County Court Fees Order 1999	S.I. 1999/689
The County Court Fees (Amendment) Order 1999	S.I. 1999/2548
The County Court Fees (Amendment) Order 2000	S.I. 2000/639
The County Court Fees (Amendment) Order 2003	S.I. 2003/648
The County Court Fees (Amendment) Order 2004	S.I. 2004/2098
The County Court Fees (Amendment No. 2) Order 2000	S.I. 2000/939
The County Court Fees (Amendment No. 2) Order 2003	S.I. 2003/718
The County Court Fees (Amendment No. 4) Order 2000	S.I. 2000/2310

NOTES ON TEXT

The text printed above incorporates the following amendments:

art. 3 amended by Civil Proceedings Fees (Amendment) (No. 2) Order 2007 (SI 2007/2176), art. 3;

art. 4 substituted by Civil Proceedings Fees (Amendment) (No. 2) Order 2007 (SI 2007/2176), art. 4;

sch. 1 substituted by Civil Proceedings Fees (Amendment) (No. 2) Order 2007 (SI 2007/2176), art. 5 and sch. amended by Civil Proceedings Fees (Amendment) (No. 2) (Amendment) Order 2007 (SI 2007/2801);

sch. 1A inserted by Civil Proceedings Fees (Amendment) (No. 2) Order 2007 (SI 2007/2176), art. 5 and sch.

Non-Contentious Probate Fees Order 2004

As from 1 October 2007, amended by the Non-Contentious Probate Fees (Amendment) Order 2007 (SI 2007/2174). Articles 4 and 5 are replaced by:

4 Remission of Fees

Schedule 1A applies for the purpose of ascertaining whether a party is entitled to a remission or part remission of a fee prescribed by this Order.

5

The Lord Chancellor may, on the ground of financial hardship or for other reasonable cause, remit in whole or in part any fee prescribed by this Order.

A new sch. 1A is inserted after sch. 1:

SCHEDULE 1A   REMISSION OF FEES

[Schedule introduced by art. 4]

1 Interpretation

(1) In this Schedule—

'child care costs' and 'the Independent Living Funds' have the meaning given to them in the Criminal Defence Service (Financial Eligibility) Regulations 2006;

'child' means a child of the party, living in his household, under the age of 18;

'couple' has the meaning given in section 3(5A) of the Tax Credits Act 2002;

'disposable monthly income' has the meaning given in paragraph 3;

'excluded benefits' means—

(a) any of the following benefits payable under the Social Security Contributions and Benefits Act 1992—

    (i) attendance allowance paid under section 64;

    (ii) severe disablement allowance;

    (iii) carer's allowance;

    (iv) disability living allowance;

    (v) constant attendance allowance paid under section 104 or paragraph 4 or 7(2) of Schedule 8 as an increase to a disablement pension;

    (vi) council tax benefit;

    (vii) any payment made out of the social fund;

    (viii) housing benefit;

(b) any direct payments made under the Community Care, Services for Carers and Children's Services (Direct Payments) (England) Regulations 2003 or the Community Care, Services for Carers and Children's Services (Direct Payments) (Wales) Regulations 2004;

(c) a back to work bonus payable under section 626 of the Jobseekers Act 1995;

(d) any exceptionally severe disablement allowance paid under the Personal Injuries (Civilians) Scheme 1983;

(e) any pensions paid under the Naval, Military and Air Forces etc (Disablement and Death) Service Pension Order 2006;

(f) any payments made from the Independent Living Funds; and

(g) any financial support paid under an agreement for the care of a foster child;

'gross monthly income' means total monthly income, for the month in which the application for remission or part remission is made, from all sources other than receipt of any of the excluded benefits;

'partner' means a person with whom the party lives as a couple and includes a person with whom the party is not currently living but from whom he is not living separate and apart;

'party' means the party who would, but for this Schedule, be liable to pay the fee required under this Order.

2 Remission or Part Remission of Fees

(1) No fee shall be payable under this Order by a party if, at the time when the fee would otherwise be payable, his disposable monthly income is £50 or less.

(2) The maximum amount of fee payable by a party is—
    (a) if his disposable monthly income is more than £50 but does not exceed £210, an amount equal to one-quarter of every £10 of his disposable monthly income up to a maximum of £50; and
    (b) if his disposable monthly income is more than £210, an amount equal to £50 plus one-half of every £10 over £200 of his disposable monthly income.

(3) Where the fee that would otherwise be payable under this Order is greater than the maximum fee which a party is required to pay as calculated in sub-paragraph (2), the fee shall be remitted to the amount payable under that sub-paragraph.

3 Disposable Monthly Income

(1) A party's disposable monthly income is his gross monthly income for the month in which the fee becomes payable ('the period') less the deductions referred to in subparagraphs (2) and (3).

(2) There are to be deducted from the gross monthly income—
    (a) income tax paid or payable in respect of the period;
    (b) any contributions estimated to have been paid under Part I of the Social Security Contributions and Benefits Act 1992;
    (c) either—
        (i) monthly rent or monthly payment in respect of a mortgage debt or hereditable security, payable by him in respect of his only or main dwelling, less any housing benefit paid under the Social Security Contributions and Benefits Act 1992; or
        (ii) the monthly cost of his living accommodation;
    (d) any child care costs paid or payable in respect of the period;
    (e) if the party is making bona fide payments for the maintenance of a child who is not a member of his household, the amount of such payments paid or payable in respect of the period;
    (f) any amount paid or payable, in respect of the period, in pursuance of a court order.

(3) There shall be deducted from the gross monthly income an amount representing the cost of living expenses in respect of the period being—
    (a) £279; plus
    (b) £198 for each child of the party; plus
    (c) £142, if the party has a partner.

4 Resources of Partners

(1) For the purpose of determining whether a party is entitled to the remission or part remission of a fee in accordance with this Schedule, the income of his partner, if any, is to be included as income of the party.

(2) The receipt by a partner of a qualifying benefit does not entitle a party to remission of a fee.

5 Application for Remission of Fees

(1) An application for remission or part remission of a fee shall be made to the court officer at the time when the fee would otherwise be payable.

(2) The applicant must provide documentary evidence of—
    (a) such of his gross monthly income as he derives from—
        (i) employment;
        (ii) rental or other income received from persons living with him by reason of their residence in his home;
        (iii) a pension; or
        (iv) a state benefit, not being an excluded benefit;
    (b) any expenditure being deducted from his gross monthly income in accordance with paragraph 3(2).

Supplement to Appendix 6
Selected Legislation

In the supplements to appendices 1 to 6 notes by the editors of *Blackstone's Civil Practice* are in italic type and the text of legislation is in upright type.

Community Legal Service (Costs) Regulations 2000

Amendments are made by the Community Legal Service (Costs) (Amendment) Regulations 2007 (SI 2007/2444) as from 1 October 2007.

In reg. 2, the definition of Regional Director *is deleted and the following definition is inserted:*

'Director' means any Director appointed by the Commission in accordance with the Funding Code and any other person authorised to act on his behalf, except a supplier;

In regs 10, 13, 20 and 23 Regional Director *is changed to* Director *wherever it appears.*

Housing Act 1996

As from 6 April 2007, a new s. 153A is substituted by the Police and Justice Act 2006, s. 26:

153A Anti-social Behaviour Injunction

(1) In this section—
'anti-social behaviour injunction' means an injunction that prohibits the person in respect of whom it is granted from engaging in housing-related anti-social conduct of a kind specified in the injunction;
'anti-social conduct' means conduct capable of causing nuisance or annoyance to some person (who need not be a particular identified person);
'conduct' means conduct anywhere;
'housing-related' means directly or indirectly relating to or affecting the housing management functions of a relevant landlord.
(2) The court on the application of a relevant landlord may grant an anti-social behaviour injunction if the condition in subsection (3) is satisfied.
(3) The condition is that the person against whom the injunction is sought is engaging, has engaged or threatens to engage in housing-related conduct capable of causing a nuisance or annoyance to—
  (a) a person with a right (of whatever description) to reside in or occupy housing accommodation owned or managed by a relevant landlord,
  (b) a person with a right (of whatever description) to reside in or occupy other housing accommodation in the neighbourhood of housing accommodation mentioned in paragraph (a),
  (c) a person engaged in lawful activity in, or in the neighbourhood of, housing accommodation mentioned in paragraph (a), or
  (d) a person employed (whether or not by a relevant landlord) in connection with the exercise of a relevant landlord's housing management functions.
(4) Without prejudice to the generality of the court's power under subsection (2), a kind of conduct may be described in an anti-social behaviour injunction by reference to a person or persons and, if it is, may (in particular) be described by reference—

(a) to persons generally,

(b) to persons of a description specified in the injunction, or

(c) to persons, or a person, specified in the injunction.

As from 6 April 2007, amendments are made by the Police and Justice Act 2006, sch. 14, para. 32. In s. 153C(1)(b) and s. 154(1)(b), section 153A(4) is replaced by any of paragraphs (a) to (d) of section 153A(3).

Index